COOPERATIVE
LEARNING

Research on Teaching Monograph Series

COOPERATIVE LEARNING

Robert E. Slavin
JOHNS HOPKINS UNIVERSITY

Longman

New York & London

COOPERATIVE LEARNING

Longman Inc., 1560 Broadway, New York, N.Y. 10036
Associated companies, branches, and representatives
throughout the world.

Developmental Editor: Nicole Benevento
Editorial and Production Supervisor: Ferne Y. Kawahara
Manufacturing Supervisor: Marion Hess

Library of Congress Cataloging in Publication Data

Slavin, Robert E.
  Cooperative learning.

  (Research on teaching monograph series)
  Bibliography: p.
  Includes index.
  1. Group work in education. 2. Educational
innovations. I. Title. II. Series.
LB1032.S54 1983   371.3'95   82–16188
ISBN 0-582-28355-8

Manufactured in the United States of America

To my parents

Contents

Acknowledgments

I would like to thank the many people who read various drafts of this book and provided valuable comments and criticisms, including Noreen Webb, Spencer Kagan, Nancy Madden, William Zangwill, Mary Rohrkemper, Michael Cook, and Joseph Slavin. I'd also like to thank Hazel Kennedy and Barbara Hucksoll for their help with typing the manuscript.

Much of the research reviewed in this book was conducted at Johns Hopkins University under funding from the National Institute of Education (Grant No. NIE-G-80-0113) and the Office of Special Education (Grant No. G008001494), U.S. Department of Education. However, the opinions expressed are mine, and do not represent Department of Education policy.

Robert Slavin

1

An Introduction to Cooperative Learning

Whenever a teacher plans a lesson or an entire course, or when a researcher or developer creates a new instructional method, they must choose a means of organizing their instruction from among a range of options, given the real-life constraints of the classroom setting. Once a decision is made on what is to be taught, the teacher or researcher must decide how this material is to be taught. This decision lies at the heart of teaching and of teaching research. The *instructional system*, the means by which information and skills are transmitted to students, is the critical feature of school organization. All other elements of school organization must ultimately be directed at making the basic instructional system applied at the classroom level as effective as possible for all students.

The essential elements of the instructional system can be summarized in two categories: the instructional *task structure* and the student *incentive structure*. The task structure refers to the many ways in which the teacher (or students themselves) sets up activities designed to result in student learning. A teacher may choose between lecture, individual seatwork, or group seatwork; unitary, subgrouped, or individualized instructional pacing; written or oral student responses; frequent or infrequent tests; and so on. Recent research on teaching has been largely directed at examining the learning outcomes of a wide range of alternative instructional task structures (see, for example, Bossert, 1977; Brophy, 1979; Good and Grouws, 1979).

However, to describe the classroom task structure is not sufficient to explain how the instructional system produces student learning. If students are not motivated to learn, the particular task structure being used will make little difference. The term *incentive structure* is used to refer to the means of motivating students to perform learning tasks. The classroom incentive structure refers primarily to the grading system, but also includes day-to-day means of motivating students to be prepared and to pay attention in class, such as methods of calling on students, feedback to students, and classroom behavior management.

The essentials of the traditional instructional system are so similar from school to school and even from country to country that we often forget that there is nothing sacred or immutable about them. With regard to task structures, most teachers use some combination of lectures, discussions, individual seatwork, small homogeneous groups working with the teacher, and individual tests (see, for example, Sirotnik, 1982). Students are rarely allowed, and even less often encouraged, to help one another with their work; in most schools, peer relationships during school hours are largely restricted to the playground and lunchroom. The almost universal incentive structure used is a grading system, in which students compete for a limited number of good grades. Even when grading is not done on a strict "curve," the fact that few teachers would be willing to give all their students "A's" or "F's" indicates that there is a competition for a limited number of good grades.

Is the optimal instructional system to be found in the range of variation seen among traditional classrooms? Perhaps; maybe the durability and universality of these methods stem from their effectiveness. However, this is an empirical question. For example, the traditional incentive system, normative grading, seems to be far from optimal. Expectancy theory (see, for example, Kukla, 1972) contends that motivation to perform a given task is a product of the incentive value of success (i.e., the importance to the individual of succeeding), and the probability of success given effort. Effort is held to be at a maximum when achieving a particular goal is neither too easy nor impossibly difficult. Yet a norm-referenced grading system virtually insures that some students will have very little chance of success, while making success easy for other students. Also, by putting students in competition with one another, both for day-to-day praise and for grades, the traditional incentive system makes helping and encouragement among students unlikely, and may lead to anti-academic norms among many students. This phenomenon was discussed at length by Coleman (1961), who documented the low value of academic success to the peer group and contrasted it to the high value of sports success. Coleman noted that in sports, success reflects well on others, where in academics, success is had only at the expense of others, and concluded that these differences in the consequences for peers of individual success at least partly explained the different values placed by student peer groups on sports and academics.

Traditional task structures may also be less than optimal for student achievement. As much as research indicates the importance of active participation on the part of students (see, for example, Good & Grouws, 1979), the fact that there is only one teacher for thirty or more students in most classrooms means that the percentage of class time during which students can actively participate is low. It may be that structuring other kinds of interaction, for instance student-student interaction, could provide more of an opportunity for students to take an active part in their learning.

Cooperative Learning

This book is about a set of alternatives to the traditional instructional system: cooperative learning methods. These are techniques that use cooperative *task structures*, in which students spend much of their class time working in 4–6 member heterogeneous groups. They also use cooperative *incentive structures*, in which students earn recognition, rewards, or (occasionally) grades based on the academic performance of their groups. Research on cooperation has been conducted since the beginning of this century (see Maller, 1929), although classroom research on practical cooperative methods began in the early 1970s. This classroom research is now quite extensive. It has taken place in inner-city, suburban, and rural schools from California to Israel, in grades from two to twelve, and in such subjects as mathematics, language arts, social studies, and reading. There are several cooperative learning methods, which vary in almost every particular, including the philosophies of their creators and the research methods they use to explore their effects. What unites them is their applications of the basic principles of cooperative incentive and task structures to achieve cognitive as well as non-cognitive goals in typical classrooms. The cooperative learning researchers are also united in their belief that the optimal instructional system may not be found within the range of variation among traditional classrooms, but must be created based on sound psychological and pedagogical theory and rigorously evaluated in classroom practice.

This book presents the theoretical basis of cooperative learning, the methods based on this theory, and the results of evaluations of these methods. It is in one sense an interim report on cooperative learning research, as this research is continuing and expanding; new researchers will bring new perspectives to this effort, and many of the conclusions drawn here will be questioned or overturned. However, there is a sufficient basis for a statement of the state of the art in cooperative learning research, and describing this state of the art is the purpose of this book.

What Is Cooperation?

The term "cooperation" can refer to four quite distinct things. It can refer to *cooperative behavior*, such as working with or helping others. It can refer to a *cooperative incentive structure* (Slavin, 1977a) in which a group of two or more individuals are rewarded based on the performance of all group members. Cooperation often refers to *cooperative task structures*, in which a group of two or more individuals can or must work together but may or may not receive rewards based on their group's performance. Finally, it can refer to *cooperative motives*, the predisposition to act cooperatively or altruistically in a situation that allows individuals a choice between cooperative, competitive, or individualistic behavior. Presence of cooperative incentive or task structures or of cooperative motives does not guarantee that cooperative behavior will occur, so it is important to distinguish cooperative behavior as one possible outcome of cooperative incentive or task structures or of cooperative motives, rather than as synonymous with them.

Cooperative behavior refers to actual participation and coordination of efforts between two or more individuals. The essential ingredient of cooperative behavior is the attempt of each cooperator to facilitate the task performance or goal attainment of his or her fellow cooperators. This almost always requires coordination of efforts between individuals, where communication between cooperators is critical. For example, if two people are building a house together, they must find a way to divide tasks, coordinate their activities, jointly plan a sequence of tasks, and pay close attention to what each other is doing.

The alternatives to cooperative behavior are individualistic behavior, where individuals operate independently of one another, and competitive behavior, where individuals attempt to hinder one another's task behaviors. Most competitive incentive structures do not involve competitive (i.e., hindering) behaviors. When two gas stations are in a price war, they compete by lowering prices (an individualistic behavior), but not by attempting to hinder their competitors from doing their job. If students are competing for good grades, they most often compete by studying (an individualistic behavior) rather than by trying to keep their classmates from studying, although there are cases in which competition for grades does lead to hindering, as when students steal required books from the library or spoil each other's science experiments.

It is sometimes inferred that cooperative behavior is good (or prosocial) and competitive behavior is bad (or anti-social). However, it is impossible to put value judgments on cooperative or competitive behavior without knowledge of the context. For example, price fixing and cheating (sharing answers) on examinations are cooperative behaviors; playing tennis or chess involve competitive behaviors (although they also involve cooperative behaviors, as the competitors must both participate and coordinate their activities to experience the pleasure of playing the games). Group competition is a form of cooperative behavior, because the group members must participate and coordinate their activities to accomplish their goals (which happen to be defined as out-performing another group). Examples of group competitions include volleyball, writing grant proposals, party politics, organized crime, and war. As these examples illustrate, cooperative behaviors as such are not morally superior or inherently more pro-social than competitive behaviors.

What defines a *cooperative incentive structure* is that two or more individuals are in a situation where the task-related efforts of any individual helps others to be rewarded. For example, if three people traveling in a car help push the car out of the mud, all of them benefit from each other's efforts (by being able to continue their trip). A football team is also a cooperative incentive structure, even though the team as a whole is in competition with other teams. This is true because for any individual team member to win, the entire team must win, and this in turn depends on the efforts of the other team members.

It is possible to have a cooperative incentive structure without the members actually working together to achieve a common goal. In a wrestling team, each wrestler competes with an opponent in his own weight class, and the team score is the total number of wins. Even though the team members cannot directly help one another to wrestle, they can be on a winning team only if most of their teammates win. Similarly, when researchers contribute chapters to an edited volume, they are in a cooperative incentive structure even if they have never met, because each researcher's contribution helps the entire group to be rewarded through the successful completion of the entire volume. A cooperative incentive structure can exist without the actual occurrence of cooperative behavior. Two typists might be rewarded based on the sum of their output, but they cannot help each other type, because typing does not lend itself to collaborative activity. A football player who is angry with his coach might refuse to play, but he is still in a cooperative incentive structure because if the team wins, he wins.

The alternatives to the cooperative incentive structure are *competitive* and *individualistic* incentive structures (see Johnson and Johnson, 1974). In a competitive incentive structure, individuals are in *negative interdependence* for rewards (Michaels, 1977). That is, for one person to be successful, another must fail. A competitive reward structure always involves scarce resources, such as money, recognition, affection, etc. For example, in a chess game, "winning" is a resource that is available to only one of the two individuals who want it. (But note that chess is also a cooperative reward structure in that both players receive the pleasure of playing only if the other will play with them.) Submitting articles to most academic journals is of course a competitive incentive structure that does not involve face-to-face competition.

In an individualistic incentive structure, one person's performance has no consequences for the chances of others to succeed. For example, if Mr. Smith plants a garden for his own consumption, it makes no difference to him whether his neighbors' gardens succeed or fail.

Cooperative task structures are situations in which two or more individuals are allowed, encouraged, or required to work together on some task. Some tasks require cooperative activity by their nature; for example, dancing the fox-trot, seesawing, carrying a sofa, or staging a production of *Hamlet* absolutely require the participation of two or more persons and require that they coordinate their activities. Other tasks lend themselves to cooperation, but could be done by individuals. For example, one person can carry a five-meter board, but two can do it much more easily. One detective might be able to solve a crime, but two or more can probably do it more quickly and effectively. In such cases, the nature of the task is likely to lead to cooperative behavior if task completion is important to the individuals involved and if the individuals are not under a reward structure that interferes with their motivation to cooperate. For example, the detectives might not choose to cooperate to solve the crime if they are in competition for a promotion.

Cooperative task structures can also exist when cooperation itself is allowed, expected, or reinforced. For example, a teacher might simply tell students that they may work together if they wish. Another might tell students that they are *expected* to work together, either in pairs or in small groups. A third might reinforce students for exhibiting cooperative behavior, by praising students when they work together or by giving them points for doing so in the context of a behavior modification plan.

Many cooperative tasks involve specialization of functions. It would be possible for one person to write this book, type it, edit it, set it in type, run it on a printing press, bind it, and hawk it in the streets, but it is much more efficient to set up a cooperative relationship between the author, a typist, a typesetter, a binder, and a publisher to get the job done more effectively. On the other hand, some cooperative tasks do not lend themselves to specialization. For example, when two people must lift one big rock, there is no way to divide up responsibilities.

The alternative to a cooperative task structure is an independent task structure, in which mutual assistance is impossible or forbidden. An example of an inherently individual task structure is swimming; someone can help you learn the breast stroke, but no one can help you do it. Typing is another inherently independent task structure. Working on worksheets in school is not inherently an independent task, but a teacher can make it an independent task structure by forbidding students to work together or by punishing them for doing so.

A fourth concept relating to cooperation is *cooperative motives*, such as predispositions to act cooperatively or altruistically instead of competitively or individualistically, or preference for cooperative activities over competitive or individualistic ones. In some situations, some individuals may choose to exhibit cooperative behaviors, while others choose competitive or individualistic behaviors. The predisposition to cooperate, a personality variable, may also influence the occurrence or non-occurrence of cooperative behavior, regardless of (or in interaction with) the reward and task structures.

Few cooperative incentives or task structures or cooperative behaviors or motives are pure in the real world. A member of a basketball team may be cooperating with her teammates to win the game, but competing with her opponents, and even competing with her own teammates for individual recognition. The choice between being a good "team player" or going for individual glory is a common theme in sports and sports literature. In a marriage, the couple may cooperate in thousands of ways on childrearing, handling finances, dividing housework, making money, and so on, but both partners are also trying to satisfy their individual needs that sometimes must be satisfied at the expense of their spouse's needs, as might be the case when one has a job offer in a distant city. No matter how altruistic or helpful persons are toward others, they must also meet their own needs as well. In fact, there are few if any purely cooperative situations that arise in real life; individuals in cooperation with one another must also weigh the degree to which their individual needs are being met, and this often places cooperating persons in competition with one another over scarce resources that meet their individual needs. In fact, we sometimes even compete to be the best cooperator, as when children fight for the privilege of cleaning the blackboard.

EFFECTS OF COOPERATION: LABORATORY RESEARCH

The issue of cooperative vs. competitive incentive structures is one of the oldest themes in social psychology. Research on this topic was already well developed by the 1920s (Maller, 1929). However, until recently this research was done in brief studies either in social psychological laboratories or, more commonly, in contrived field settings that resembled the laboratory. In this book, studies that were implemented over periods of less than two weeks in any setting are referred to as "laboratory" studies. While these brief studies tend to be too limited in external validity to be useful as *evaluations* of cooperative learning methods for use in classrooms, they have provided much of the theoretical basis on which the practical cooperative learning programs and research on these programs are based. This chapter does not presume to review the hundreds of laboratory studies on cooperation and competition, but quickly reviews the major findings relevant to building the theoretical base from which research on practical cooperative learning methods derives its conceptual framework.

Effects of Cooperation on Performance. Despite the many studies conducted to find the effects of cooperation on performance, these effects are still rather poorly understood. Four recent reviews completely disagreed on the direction of the effect. Johnson and Johnson (1974) summarized the research by stating that cooperation is better than competition or individualization for all but the most concrete, repetitive tasks. In a later meta-analysis, Johnson, Maruyama, Johnson, Nelson, and Skon (1981) suggested that the evidence supporting cooperative incentive structures over competitive and individualistic ones in increasing productivity is so strong that further research on this comparison is unnecessary. However, Michaels (1977) reviewed much of the same literature and concluded that competition is usually better than cooperation for most tasks. Slavin (1977a) held that over the brief duration of a laboratory study, cooperation is more effective in increasing performance when coordination of efforts is vital to effective functioning, while competition is at least as effective as cooperation when coordination of efforts is not so important. Since most tasks of practical importance (including learning) do not *require* coordination of efforts between two or more individuals, this conclusion was closer to Michaels (1977) than to Johnson and Johnson (1974) or Johnson et al. (1981). However, Slavin (1977a) held that over longer periods, growth of social pressures favoring performance in cooperative groups makes cooperation more effective. A similar conclusion was reached in a different form by Miller and Hamblin (1963), who postulated that cooperative reward structures were most effective for interdependent (cooperative) task structures, but least effective for independent tasks.

To understand the controversy over the laboratory evidence concerning the effects of cooperative incentive structures on performance, it is important to have a casual model linking cooperative incentive structures with enhanced performance. The following sections develop such a model.

Does Help Help?   The most obvious effect of a cooperative incentive structure should be to get individuals to help one another. This is so apparent that most studies have not measured it, but those that have done so have always found more helping under a cooperative incentive than under an individual or competitive one (Deutsch, 1949a; Slavin, 1980a; Johnson and Johnson, 1981). However, while it appears likely that cooperative incentives would increase helping among group members, it is not so clear that helping per se always increases performance. In fact, it is obvious that on many tasks, such as typing, running, or swimming, helping during the task performance is impossible, or of little value, while on other tasks, such as carrying heavy loads, taking tests, or solving difficult problems, helping is likely to lead to a better group product. Two similar studies illustrate this dichotomy. Klugman (1944) had small groups of children do arithmetic problems under a cooperative contingency in which the groups received rewards based on the number of problems they could do accurately, with no time limit. He contrasted this condition with one in which children worked for individual rewards based on the number of problems they could work correctly. The group under the cooperative condition got significantly more problems right. In a similar study, DeCharms (1957) found exactly the opposite relationship; the children who worked independently got more correct answers on the arithmetic problems than did those working under the cooperative incentive. There was a critical difference between the studies; while Klugman (1944) allowed the children unlimited time, DeCharms (1957) set a time limit and told his subjects to concentrate on speed. In the Klugman study, students were able to pool their knowledge to improve the performance of all group members; in the DeCharms study, "helping" was of little value, and might have even slowed the subjects down.

Thus, while it is clear that under certain conditions cooperative incentives lead to increased helping behavior, *the degree to which help is valuable for performance depends on the task and outcome measure*. Most of the tasks used in the laboratory research on cooperation, competition, and individualization for which cooperation produces the highest performance are problem-solving tasks for which two (or more) heads are obviously better than one. For example, Miller and Hamblin (1963) gave each of four subjects three unique numbers between one and thirteen. The task was to find the missing number. Since the four subjects had twelve numbers between them, they only had to share their numbers to find the missing one, and they did share more readily when they received a group reward based on how fast they could find the answer than when they were in competition to find the answer first, where sharing would simply help others to win. Literally dozens of studies have shown that two or more individuals working together can figure out a maze or a concept underlying a set of numbers or words faster than can individuals working alone (e.g., Lemke, Randle, and Robertshaw, 1969; Gurnee, 1968; Laughlin, McGlynn, Anderson, and Jacobson, 1968). When two or more individuals take a test together, they do better than when they work separately (e.g., Laughlin and Johnson, 1966; R. T. Johnson and D. W. Johnson, 1979). Many studies have shown that two or more individuals can solve problems of various kinds better when they work in groups than when they work independently (e.g., Deutsch, 1949a; Hammond and Goldman, 1961; Thorndike, 1938).

On the kinds of tasks used in the studies cited above, groups *obviously* score better than individuals. In the problem-solving studies, groups would have outscored individuals even if more able group members solved the problems by themselves, because the less able group members would have still been assigned the group score. As early as the 1930s, Thorndike (1938) considered the superiority of group to individual problem solving to have been proved, and proposed that further research go beyond that rather obvious finding to explore on what kinds of tasks groups do best. In fact, in many of the studies cited above, it was assumed at the beginning that groups would outperform individuals and some issue beyond groups vs. individual problem solving was the focus of the study.

A few studies examined the reasons that groups did better on problem-solving tasks, and concluded that they did better simply because they pooled the problem-solving abilities of their members. Faust (1959), Marquart (1955), and Ryack (1965) compared groups that really worked together to "nominal" groups. The nominal group scores were created by randomly assigning subjects who had actually worked alone to artificial "groups," and crediting all "group" members with having solved a problem if any one of them solved the problem. In all three studies, the real groups had much higher scores than the individuals, but not than the "nominal" groups, suggesting that the real groups had high scores not because of their interaction or motivation but because if any individual could solve the problem, their groupmates would get credit for it, regardless of their own participation or learning.

Another category of tasks on which cooperation is obviously more efficient than competition is studies in which the competition is likely to disrupt performance. The classic example of this is the Mintz (1951) experiment, in which the task was for several individuals to pull cones on strings out of a milk bottle whose neck would permit only one cone to be withdrawn at a time. Under cooperative instructions (get all the cones out as quickly as possible), the individuals arranged to take turns, and quickly got all the cones out, but under non-cooperative instructions (get your own cone out as quickly as possible), the traffic jam at the mouth of the bottle increased everyone's time. In another study of this kind, Graziano, French, Brownell, and Hartup (1976) gave children stacks of blocks. The children were assigned to groups of three. In a cooperative condition, the children built a tower together, and were rewarded based on total number of blocks in the tower. In a non-cooperative condition, children also built a single tower, but they were rewarded based on the number of their *own* blocks they could get onto the tower. In the condition in which children were trying to get their own blocks into the tower, the towers fell more often and ultimately included fewer blocks than in the condition in which children were concerned only with increasing the total number of blocks in the tower.

When hindering is a likely outcome of a competitive task or reward structure, and cooperative instructions or rewards remove the hindering, cooperation will, of course, improve group performance. Many studies comparing cooperation and competition are of this type (see, for example, Crombag, 1966; Raven and Eachus, 1963).

A study using methods similar to those used by Graziano et al. (1976) demonstrated how critical the hindering that resulted from competition was in explaining their results. Rosenbaum, Moore, Cotton, Cook, Hieser, Shovar, and Gray (1980) replicated the Graziano et al. (1976) findings, but found no differences between cooperative, competitive, and independent incentive conditions when the subjects built their *own* towers in all conditions but received rewards in different ways.

Group Productivity vs. Individual Learning.   The kind of performance of interest in this book bears little relationship to building towers of blocks, pulling cones out of bottles, or even to problem solving in the sense studied in the experiments discussed above. Learning is a completely individual outcome that may or may not be improved by cooperation, but it is clearly not obviously improved by cooperation the way problem-solving performance of the kind described above is. Leonard Bernstein and the author of this book could write a brilliant concerto together, about twice as good as the average of the concertos he and I would write working separately (since I can barely read music). But how much did we learn from working cooperatively? I doubt that Leonard Bernstein would learn much about writing concertos from me, and I might do better to take a course on music than to start by watching a composer write a concerto. The point of this example is to illustrate that *learning is completely different from "group" productivity*. It may well be that working in a group under certain circumstances does increase the learning of the individuals in that group more than would working under other arrangements, but a measure of group productivity provides no evidence one way or the other on this; only an individual learning measure that cannot be influenced by group member help can indicate which incentive or task structure is best. Learning takes place only between the ears of the learner. If a group produces a beautiful lab report, but only a few students really contributed to it, it is unlikely that the group as a whole learned more than they might have learned had they each had to write his or her own (perhaps less beautiful) lab reports under an individualistic or competitive incentive structure. In fact, what often happens in cooperative groups that produce a single report, worksheet, or other group product is that the most able group members simply do the work or give the answers to their groupmates, which may be the most efficient strategy for group productivity, but is a poor strategy for individual learning. There are several studies in which productivity measures were at variance with learning outcomes. Haines and McKeachie (1967) found that psychology students in large discussion groups covered a larger number of questions under cooperative incentives than under competitive ones, but the groups did not differ in examination performance. Smith, Madden, and Sobel (1957) found more ideas expressed in a cooperative discussion group than in a competitively structured group, but there were no differences in recall of the material discussed. Johnson, Johnson, Johnson, and Anderson (1976) and Johnson, Johnson, and Scott (1978) found that students who worked cooperatively and then took a test on which they could help each other performed much better than did students who worked alone and took the tests by themselves. However, when the tests were given to the cooperative students individually, they did no better than the individual students in one study (Johnson, Johnson, Johnson, and Anderson, 1976) and worse than the individual students in the other (Johnson, Johnson, and Scott, 1978).

Because it makes sense only at the individual level, learning is a performance measure that resembles "means-independent" tasks studied in many social psychological laboratory studies. In these studies, the evidence does not clearly favor cooperative incentives (Miller and Hamblin, 1963). The DeCharms (1957) study of timed arithmetic problems discussed earlier is one example of a study in which subjects could do little to help one another, and no differences between cooperative and competitive incentives were found. When differences favoring cooperative incentive structures are found on tasks on which helping is forbidden or useless, it is usually because a cooperative incentive is being compared to no incentive at all. For example, Hurlock (1927) found that students worked more individual arithmetic problems when they worked in teams trying to "beat" another team than when they simply were asked to work problems by themselves with no incentive. However, when both groups received some reward, cooperative and competitive incentive structures tended to produce equal performance (e.g., Busching and Busching, in press; Seta, Paulus, and Schkade, 1976) or competition actually exceeded cooperation in effects on performance (e.g., Weinstein and Holzbach, 1972; Scott and Cherrington, 1974; Bruning, Sommer, and Jones, 1966).

In their recent meta-analysis entitled "Effects of Cooperative, Competitive, and Individualistic Goal Structures on Achievement," Johnson, Maruyama, Johnson, Nelson, and Skon (1981) reviewed 122 studies. Their conclusion, based on this review, was as follows: "the overall effects stand as strong evidence for the superiority of cooperation in promoting achievement and productivity. . . . Given the general dissatisfaction with the level of competence achieved by students in the public school system, educators may wish to considerably increase the use of cooperative learning procedures to promote higher student achievement" (Johnson et al., 1981, p. 58). This unequivocal conclusion, based on a substantial difference in effect size favoring cooperative over individualistic and competitive incentive structures, would appear to make the cautions discussed in this chapter concerning the effects of cooperation on learning irrelevant. However, despite the title, only about 40 of the 122 studies reviewed involved comparisons of cooperative to competitive or individualistic methods with *individual achievement* as a dependent variable. The great majority of the studies compared group productivity to individual productivity on tasks on which group productivity was obviously more effective, such as solving mazes, number problems, scrambled words, and so on. In one study, the dependent variable was scores in a card game, in which cooperating individuals could share cards to get a higher score (Workie, 1974). One (Bjorkland, Johnson, and Krotee, 1980) involved golf performance, and another (Martino and Johnson, 1979) involved swimming, and compared the number of swimming skills gained by two learning-disabled students who learned cooperatively to those gained by two learning-disabled students who learned individualistically. Many of the studies involved building block towers, manipulating apparatus, judging weights, and other tasks minimally related to school achievement (e.g., Graziano et al., 1976; Raven and Eachus, 1963; Gordon, 1924). Of the studies that did involve achievement, many simply found that two or more students who take a test together do better than students who work alone (e.g., Garibaldi, 1979; Hudgins, 1960; D. W. Johnson and R. T. Johnson, 1979; Johnson, Johnson, Johnson, and Anderson, 1976; Johnson, Johnson, and Scott, 1978; Johnson, Johnson, and Skon, 1979; Laughlin and Bitz, 1975; Laughlin, Branch, and Johnson, 1969). Thus, the net direction of the effects of cooperative, competitive, and individualistic incentive and task structures per se on individual learning is still an open question, and is certainly not resolved by the Johnson et al. (1981) meta-analysis.

The purpose of the foregoing discussion was to illustrate the observation that the evidence of the laboratory and brief field studies is inconclusive with respect to the effects of helping per se on individual learning. Clearly, studies of group productivity or other studies in which working together is obviously more effective than working separately add little to an understanding of how different task structures affect learning, and such studies dominate the literature on cooperation, competition, and individualization. Since individual learning is an individual task, the most relevant literature for a theory of cooperation and learning would be the studies of other individual tasks, which tend to find greater performance under competitive and individualistic conditions than under cooperative conditions. However, learning is not just like typing or coding, either. For certain kinds of learning, discussion under cooperative conditions may improve subsequent individual achievement. For example, discussion of text improves students' recall of the text content more than reviewing the text alone (Slavin and Tanner, 1979). Engaging in controversy over social studies materials apparently improves recall of important concepts (R. T. Johnson and D. W. Johnson, 1979). Structured peer tutoring improves student learning in some cases, especially learning on the part of the tutor (Devin-Sheehan, Feldman, and Allen, 1976). Thus, studying in small groups may yet be more effective than solitary study for some learning tasks, but at this point the laboratory research on this is limited.

Group Norms.   However, helping between group members is not the only means by which cooperative *incentive* (as opposed to task) structures might influence individual performance. Another mediating variable that could link cooperative incentive structures to increased performance is group member support for whatever helps the group to be rewarded, or group norms favoring performance. These norms are central to Deutsch's (1949b) theory of cooperation and competition, and in his study of cooperating discussion groups he documented their occurrence (Deutsch, 1949a). Thomas (1957) also found that cooperative incentives led to peer norms favoring the performance of tasks that help the group to be rewarded. Slavin (1975) and Slavin, DeVries, and Hulten (1975) found that students in cooperative groups who gained in academic performance also gained in sociometric status in cooperative groups, while they lost status in competitive groups. Hulten and DeVries (1976), Madden and Slavin (in press), and Slavin (1978) found that students who had worked in cooperative learning groups were significantly more likely than control students to agree that their classmates wanted them to do their best. These findings indicate that peer norms do come to favor achievement as a consequence of cooperative incentive structures.

If group member norms do support performance of tasks that help the group to succeed, it seems logical that this would improve performance on the part of group members. Coleman (1961) found that in schools in which academic achievement helped a student to be accepted by the "leading crowd," the brightest students turned their attention more toward doing well academically than they did in schools in which achievement was not so well esteemed by the peer group. Student support for academic goals was also found by Brookover, Beady, Flood, Schweitzer, and Wisenbaker (1979) to be a strong predictor of student achievement, controlling for student background factors. Thus, the evidence supports a conclusion that group member helping on a group task and group member norms supporting performance are consequences of cooperative incentive structures and, under certain circumstances, may increase performance, including learning.

Diffusion of Responsibility. While the effects of group tasks and group norms favoring achievement are likely to have positive or, at worst, neutral effects on performance, there is one effect of cooperative incentives whose net impact is probably to *decrease* performance. This is the problem of diffusion of responsibility. In a cooperative group, it is often possible for individuals to be rewarded even if they themselves made little contribution to the group, or for individuals to fail to be rewarded even though they have done their utmost (see Slavin, 1977a). Laboratory science groups, in which a single lab report is produced, are good examples of this problem; some students always seem to find a way to get others to do the work. For this reason, studies in which a single product is made by a group are the most likely to show significantly greater gains in individual learning for competitive or individualistic groups than for cooperative ones (Julian and Perry, 1967; Johnson, Johnson, and Scott, 1978). Diffusion of responsibility is highest when group members can substitute for one another in performing the group task. When this is possible, some students are likely to do the minimum, hoping that their groupmates will pick up the slack. In theory, diffusion of responsibility should be a very serious problem in cooperative incentive and task structures. Again referring to expectancy theory (see Kukla, 1972), there is reason to conclude that given a reward of a certain value, the chances that an individual will try for the reward depends on the chances of being successful if he or she does try minus the chances of being successful even if he or she doesn't (see Slavin, 1978a). In a cooperative incentive structure, especially one involving a large group, the chances that any individual's extraordinary efforts will make a difference one way or the other is far less than would be the situation in an individualistic or a fair competitive structure, where extraordinary effort is more likely to pay off (see Slavin, 1977a, 1978a).

Because cooperative incentive structures are common in adult life (if not in classrooms), societies have worked out many ways to deal with the inherent problem of diffusion of responsibility. These include repeated exhortations to group members about the virtues of cooperation, or of doing whatever helps the group to be rewarded. The pep talk before the game is an example of this, as are special televised appeals by the president to conserve energy or to do anything that may not be in individuals' best interests but is in the nation's best interest (a nation is a cooperative incentive and task structure). Another way that groups combat diffusion of responsibility is to have interpersonal sanctions for doing whatever helps the group. For example, teammates cheer each other on, and express norms in favor of practicing and doing one's best. If a girl on a swimming team decides to skip practice or miss an important meet, her teammates are likely to be upset with her (much in contrast to the situation in a classroom, in which skipping school is tolerated or even encouraged by peers; see Baltimore City Schools, 1972). If group members' performances are visible to the other group members, they are likely to administer a very contingent reward/punishment system to see to it that group members are all doing their best.

In summary, individuals placed under a cooperative incentive are likely to encourage one another to do whatever helps the group to succeed and to help one another with the group task. Cooperative incentive structures are also likely to increase diffusion of responsibility, because each group member's own rewards are no longer dependent on his or her own efforts alone. While the effect of group member encouragement on performance is probably positive, the effect of helping may or may not be positive, depending on the kind of task involved. The effect of diffusion of responsibility is to reduce the chances that additional effort will be rewarded, and is thus likely to reduce performance. Cooperative task structures are hypothesized to increase performance by increasing helping among group members and by influencing group members to encourage one another to perform the group task.

FIGURE 1.1 Simple Theoretical Model of Effects of Cooperative Incentive and Task Structures on Performance

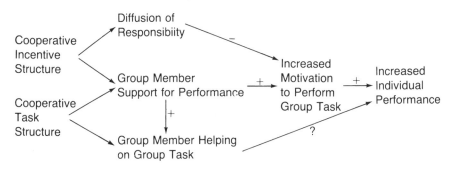

A model of how cooperative incentive and task structures might affect performance is depicted in Figure 1.1. Again, there is only one route by which cooperative incentive structures may be assumed to lead to individual motivation and thus individual performance, the route through group member support for performance. Group members' helping one another may or may not improve individual performance, depending on what the task and outcome measures are. Diffusion of responsibility, which increases as group size increases, is hypothesized to have a negative effect on individual motivation (and thus performance).

What is implied in Figure 1.1 is not, of course, that the net effect of cooperative incentive and task structures on individual performance is zero. What it is meant to convey is that the net effect depends on whether the cooperative incentive and task structures are designed to maximize the positive effects and minimize the negative ones. For example, all of the ways (described above) that group members use to reduce the effects of diffusion of responsibility essentially involve activating group member support for performance (or negative sanctions for non-performance). In structuring a group task to increase individual performance, there are many ways to activate group support for performance. For example, making group member contributions visible and quantifiable makes it possible for group members to accurately identify contributing and non-contributing members. This may be done by making the group reward depend on the sum of the members' individual performances (as in a wrestling or chess team), or by giving each member a unique subtask (as in an assembly line). Increasing the value of group rewards is likely to increase group members' motivation to apply interpersonal sanctions to motivate in turn their groupmates' efforts. The impact of helping can also be influenced by restructuring the task to improve performance under cooperative conditions. Assignment of subtasks may have this effect when the group's goal is to produce some product, as in problem-solving tasks or projects. However, when the goal is not a group product but is an individual outcome (such as learning), helping can be made more effective, for example, by training group members in effective tutoring methods or by providing materials that lend themselves to peer learning (see, for example, Slavin, Leavey, and Madden, 1982). Making the group goal and means of achieving it as clear as possible may also focus group members' efforts on effective helping.

Seen in the light of the model outlined in Figure 1.1, the results of the laboratory research are no longer inconsistent. As noted earlier in this chapter, when positive effects of cooperative incentive and task structures on performance are found the tasks involved have tended to be ones where helping is likely to improve performance and where group members can easily monitor and thereby reinforce each other's performance. Where competitive or individualistic incentives have produced greater performance, the tasks have tended to be ones on which helping is unlikely to make much difference (e.g., DeCharms, 1957) or individual group members' contributions are difficult to observe or reinforce and individuals may easily substitute for one another in performing the group task (e.g., Julian and Perry, 1967; Johnson, Johnson, and Scott, 1978).

Actually, as noted earlier, brief laboratory or field-based laboratory studies are inherently biased against cooperative incentive and task structures. Diffusion of responsibility can occur from the first minutes a group is together, contributing to an early potential decrement in performance. Helping strategies, and especially group member support and norms favoring performance, are likely to take time to develop. However, while the laboratory research on cooperative incentive and task structures has not produced performance effects that are unambiguous in general direction, it can support an understanding of the conditions under which positive or negative results are likely to be seen.

Effects of Cooperation on Interpersonal Perceptions. Achievement is not the only important outcome of schooling. Schools also play a critical part in the socialization of students to appropriate adult roles and behavior. Whether or not one believes that schools have a responsibility to concern themselves with the interpersonal skills and values of students, the fact that students spend six hours per day in school means that what goes on there will strongly influence these skills and values. When new instructional methods are proposed, their effects on socialization-related outcomes must be assessed along with their effects on achievement. The dunce cap or public caning might be effective means of threatening students and thereby improving their behavior and learning, but even if this were so, the presumably negative effects of the use of these kinds of punishment on student self-esteem and other non-cognitive outcomes would (hopefully) forbid their use.

At this point in American education, two categories of interpersonal relationships have especially great importance. These are relationships between students of different racial or ethnic groups (see Chapter 4) and relationships between mainstreamed students and their normal-progress classmates (see Chapter 5). In the case of intergroup relations, early positive expectations about what desegregation would do to improve relationships across ethnic lines have given way to a realization that as they are currently organized, desegregated schools do not of themselves increase cross-ethnic friendships or reduce "ethnic encapsulization" (Gerard and Miller, 1975; St. John, 1975; Stephan, 1978). Research on mainstreaming has discovered that despite earlier hopes, mainstreamed students remain socially isolated and rejected by many of their normal-progress classmates (see Meyers, McMillan, and Yoshida, 1980; Semmel, Gottlieb, and Robinson, 1979).

In considering the problem of improving relationships across important interpersonal barriers, cooperative small group activities have been suggested for thirty years as a potential solution (see, for example, Allport, 1954). In fact, while there is now a substantial literature on cooperative learning and both ethnic relations and attitudes toward mainstreamed students, there are few alternative strategies that have been suggested and systematically evaluated.

Although intergroup relations and relations between mainstreamed and normal-progress students are the most practically important manifestations of interpersonal relations in school, a general theory of effects of cooperative incentive and task structures on interpersonal relations is important. While the effects of cooperation on performance are complex and studies concerning these effects are inconsistent, the effects of cooperation on interpersonal relations are quite straightforward and well documented (see Johnson and Johnson, 1974; Slavin, 1977a).

Interpersonal relations can be operationalized in many ways. For example, they can be measured as the number or quality of pairwise friendships existing between members of some group. They can be measured as group cohesiveness, the degree to which the group is attractive to its members and the degree to which the group will act to maintain its membership and group identity. Interpersonal relations can also be operationalized as the extent to which individuals feel they are liked or valued by others in a group.

However interpersonal relations are defined, there are several well-established principles concerning how positive relationships are formed. The most important is that positive relationships depend on *contact* (Lott and Lott, 1965). Next door neighbors are more likely to become friends than are second-to-next door neighbors, roommates more than hallmates, squad buddies more than platoonmates, and so on.

Cooperation almost invariably increases contact. If two individuals fold sheets together over even a brief period they are likely to talk, to learn each other's names, and to become at least acquaintances. If they find they share certain worldviews or favored activities, they are likely to then become friends. Similarly, individuals who work toward a common goal, such as officemates, teammates, and work crews, tend to coordinate their activities and to find themselves in the same places at the same times often enough to allow friendships to develop.

Contact is a necessary, but not sufficient condition for friendship. It does not always lead to positive affect between people. One case in which contact is unlikely to lead to liking is one in which the individuals are in competition for something they both want very much. When an individual frustrates the goal attainment of another individual, he is relatively unlikely to make that person his friend (Burnstein and Worchel, 1962). For example, two applicants for the same job might find themselves in frequent contact, but their relationship is unlikely to be improved by the situation. Another case in which contact is less likely to lead to friendship is one in which the contact is between individuals of very different levels of status. For example, foremen and workers are less likely to become friends than are workers with other workers and foremen with other foremen, given the same levels of contact. Allport (1954) recognized the importance of non-competitive, equal status contacts as a determinant of positive race relations (see Chapter 4).

Cooperative contact between individuals occupying equal roles is a powerful producer of positive relationships. In a cooperative group, group members help each other to attain their goals or complete their tasks. This help puts the other group members in the best possible light, as we usually like people who help us get what we want (Johnson and Johnson, 1972). In a cooperative group, all a group member usually has to do to earn the affection of his groupmates is to do his best to help the group achieve its goals. If the individual is perceived to put the group's good ahead of his own gain, the group's affection for him may be boundless, as is often the case with military heroes, sports heroes (especially if they are also seen as good "team players"), and occasionally simply the undistinguished worker who plugs away for the group without a thought for him or herself. All of these individuals are liked because they help the group under a cooperative reward structure (nation, army, home team, office staff, assembly line section) to achieve its goals. More important than crowd adulation for heroes is the much more frequent formation of friendships within co-operating groups, but part of what makes these friendships is the same dynamic that creates affection toward the hero; mutual help leads to mutual liking.

One other antecedent of liking between individuals is perceived similarity (Lott and Lott, 1965). We tend to like people whom we see as like ourselves in important ways. Most people's friends resemble themselves in age, sex, race, socioeconomic status, occupation, religion, political party, general worldview, and favored activities. When apparently dissimiliar people become friends, there is usually some exceptionally strong similarity between them on some less obvious dimension. For example, in the movie "Harold and Maude," a very rich young man became friends with an impoverished old woman because of their shared bizarre interest in funerals and their strong anti-establishment attitudes.

The fact that friendships run along the lines of perceived similarity is not in itself a negative thing, but it creates some of society's most intractable problems, such as racism, sexism, and ageism. The "wall" that really creates a ghetto of any kind—be it a ghetto for blacks, for Jews, for students, or for the wealthy—is composed of common perceptions (often shared on both sides of the "wall") that those inside are completely different from those outside. This leads to development of many friendships within the group but few with "outsiders," as perceived similarity leads to positive affect, but perceived dissimilarity often leads to negative affect. At certain times in certain societies, the dominant group has tried to annihilate a dissimilar group in its midst. More often, perceived dissimilarity creates a situation of discrimination, distrust, and suspicion between groups, which occasionally erupts into serious problems.

Programs designed to improve intergroup relations often try to attack the problem by attempting to show the similarities between different groups, and thus reduce the perceived dissimilarity that acts as a barrier to positive relationships. The phenomenal success of the television show "Roots" probably lay in the fact that non-blacks could see in the struggle of blacks their own American values and, for many Americans, a common experience of past persecution, discrimination, and eventual progress. However, such lessons are probably short-lived in their effects on prejudice.

Another way to reduce perceived dissimilarity is cooperation between individuals from dissimilar backgrounds, especially cooperation that takes place over an extended period in groups with stable compositions. Such groups create a "we" feeling that, under the right circumstances, can transcend or at least reduce the perceived dissimilarity problem between members of different racial, sex, or SES backgrounds by creating a new basis for perceived similarity, membership in the cooperating group. The more important membership in the group becomes to the members, whether as a virtue of high group status, of frequent interaction, or other factors, the less perceived dissimilarity because of such personal attributes as race will interfere with friendships and the more group membership will create a new perceived similarity between formerly "dissimilar" individuals. The best example of this in schools, outside of the cooperative learning methods discussed in this book, is team sports. Black and white students who participate on integrated teams are much more likely to have friends outside of their own race groups than are their classmates who do not (Slavin and Madden, 1979).

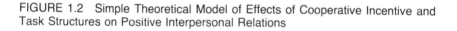

FIGURE 1.2 Simple Theoretical Model of Effects of Cooperative Incentive and Task Structures on Positive Interpersonal Relations

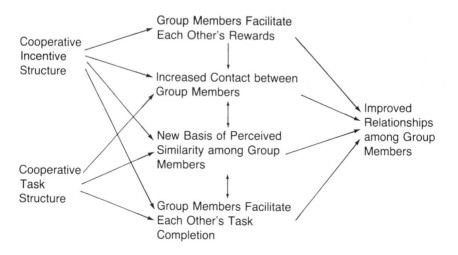

Figure 1.2 summarizes a model of how cooperative incentive and task structures might influence interpersonal relations. In this case, all of the hypothesized effects are positive; when positive effects of cooperative incentive and task structures on interpersonal relations are found, it is usually impossible to tell exactly what accounts for them, because there are so many routes by which the effect could have been mediated. Positive effects of cooperative incentive and task structures on mutual attraction measures have been found by such researchers as Scott and Cherrington (1974), Deutsch (1949a), Dunn and Goldman (1966), Grossack (1954), and Jones and Vroom (1964). Similar findings on group cohesiveness measures have been reported by Julian and Perry (1967), Phillips and D'Amico (1956), and many others, and laboratory research has supported the use of cooperative interaction to improve racial attitudes (Cook, 1978). Actually, despite the breadth and consistency of effects of cooperative incentive and task structures on interpersonal relationships, these laboratory studies probably underestimate the effects, because each of the hypothesized mediating variables between cooperation and interpersonal relations, especially contact, would presumably increase in salience and effect over time.

Effects of Cooperation on Self-Esteem. It is impossible to meaningfully measure changes in self-esteem over the short time usually allocated to a laboratory study, but this variable has been measured in many of the longer-term field experiments reported in Chapter 6. Self-esteem in school-age children has been shown by Coopersmith (1967) and others to be strongly influenced by the students' feelings that they are doing well in school and in their peer group. Since many cooperative learning methods have been found to increase student academic performance (Chapter 3) and to increase positive interpersonal relations among peers (Chapter 6), it would seem logical that they would improve student self-esteem, as students are likely (correctly) to perceive that they are doing better in school and getting along better with their peers. This model is depicted in Figure 1.3.

FIGURE 1.3   Simple Model of Effects of Cooperative Learning Methods on Student Self-Esteem

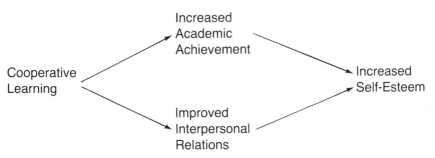

In summary, the laboratory research indicates that cooperation has potential for improving performance, mutual attraction, and self-esteem in various settings, including schools. However, the degree to which this potential can be realized depends in part on the tasks to be accomplished and the outcomes desired, and in part on the particular way in which cooperative rewards and tasks are structured. For learning outcomes in particular, cooperation could have positive or negative effects depending on how the cooperation is set up.

This book is about the cooperative learning programs used in schools to accomplish improvements in student achievement, intergroup relations, self-esteem, and other outcomes. The field experimental research reported in Chapters 3–6 finds generally positive effects of cooperative learning on these variables, but these effects are by no means uniform. One of the primary purposes of this book is to attempt to learn from the inconsistencies as well as the consistencies in the research on cooperative learning to inform a general theory of cooperation in the classroom. The potential importance of this task can hardly be overemphasized. It is clear from the writings of almost all of the researchers in the area of cooperative learning that they seriously consider cooperative learning a viable alternative to traditional instruction as the primary instructional form to be used in all schools at all levels. Such a change would represent a revolution in the socialization and instruction of students with potentially profound consequences. This book is a first attempt to explore some of these consequences in detail.

2

Cooperative Learning Methods

It is easy to criticize the instructional system used in traditional classrooms. However, proposing systematic alternatives is not so easy. In the case of applying the principles of cooperation to replace the competitive incentive structure and individualistic task structure of the traditional classroom, the most direct method would be to assign students to small groups, let them work together, and praise them based on their group product. This would solve many of the problems of the traditional classroom. However, it could create a long list of new problems. What would keep the cooperative groups from turning out like those laboratory groups in which one or two students end up doing most of the work? Why should students help each other learn—why should they care how their classmates are doing? What would keep the more able students from belittling the contributions of their lower-performing peers? How in fact could low-achieving students contribute anything important to their groups? How can students focus their studying activities to achieve the greatest possible learning for all group members? What kinds of learning materials and activities should be used with cooperative methods?

It is not enough to simply tell students to cooperate. A program based on cooperation among students must be "engineered," both to solve the problems inherent in cooperation itself and to adapt cooperative activities to the needs and limitations of the typical classroom. The following section describes the various cooperative learning methods that have been evaluated in field experiments in elementary and secondary schools. The means that the various methods have used to attempt to solve the problems inherent in cooperative learning (and in adapting cooperative learning to the typical classroom) will be discussed later in this chapter and in Chapter 3.

Cooperative Learning Methods

Student Team Learning. The most extensively researched and widely used cooperative learning techniques are the Student Team Learning methods developed by Robert Slavin, David DeVries, and Keith Edwards at Johns Hopkins University (Slavin, 1980b). Three of the student team learning methods are now in widespread use. These are *Student Teams-Achievement Divisions* (STAD), *Teams-Games-Tournament* (TGT), and *Jigsaw II*. A fourth technique, *Team Assisted Individualization* (TAI), has been more recently developed and evaluated. These methods are described below.

Student Teams-Achievement Divisions (STAD). In Student Teams-Achievement Divisions, or STAD (Slavin, 1978b), students are assigned to four- or five-member learning teams. The teams are made up of high-, average-, and low-performing students, boys and girls, and students of different racial or ethnic backgrounds, so that each team is like a microcosm of the entire class. Each week, the teacher introduces new material in a lecture or discussion. The team members then study worksheets on the material. They may work problems one at a time in pairs, take turns quizzing each other, discuss problems as a group, or use whatever means they wish to master the material. The students are given worksheet answer sheets, so it is clear to them that their task is to learn the concepts, not simply to fill out the worksheets. Team members are told that they are not finished studying until they and their teammates are sure that they understand the material.

Following team practice, students take quizzes on the materials they have been studying. Teammates may not help one another on the quizzes; at this point they are on their own. The quizzes are scored in class or soon after class. These scores are formed into team scores by the teacher.

The amount each student contributes to his or her team is determined by the amount the student's quiz score exceeds the student's own past quiz average. A base score is set five points below each student's average, and students earn points, up to a maximum of ten, for each point by which they exceed their base scores. Students with perfect papers always receive the ten-point maximum, regardless of their base scores. This individual improvement score system gives every student a good chance to contribute maximum points to the team if (and only if) the student does his or her best, and thereby shows substantial improvement or gets a perfect paper. This improvement point system has been shown to increase student academic performance even without teams (Slavin, 1980c), but it is especially important as a component of STAD since it avoids the possibility that low performing students will not be fully accepted as group members because they do not contribute many points. To illustrate this, think of a baseball team. A baseball team is a cooperative group. However, the baseball team has a serious problem: the "automatic strikeout," the team member who rarely hits the ball no matter how much he or she practices. In STAD, no one is an automatic strikeout, and by the same token no one is guaranteed success, because it is improvement that counts, and anyone is capable of improvement.

FIGURE 2.1 Example of a STAD Newsletter (from Slavin, 1980b, p. 22)

SPOTSYLVANIA ELEMENTARY SCHOOL

Issue No. 5
March 21, 1981

CALCULATORS OUTFIGURE CLASS!

The Calculators (Charlene, Alfredo, Laura, and Carl) calculated their way into first place this week, with big ten-point scores by Charlene, Alfredo, and Carl, and a near-perfect team score of 38! Their score jumped them from sixth to third in cumulative rank. Way to go Calcs! The Fantastic Four (Frank, Otis, Ursula, and Rebecca) also did a fantastic job, with Ursula and Rebecca turning in ten pointers, but the Tigers (Cissy, Lindsay, Arthur, and Willy) clawed their way from last place last week to a tie with the red-hot Four, who were second the first week, and first last week. The Fantastic Four stayed in first place in cumulative rank. The Tigers were helped out by ten-point scores from Lindsay and Arthur. The Math Monsters (Gary, Helen, Octavia, Ulysses, and Luis) held on to fourth place this week, but due to their big first-place score in the first week they're still in second place in overall rank. Helen and Luis got ten points to help the M.M.'s. Just behind the Math Monsters were the Five Alive (Carlos, Irene, Nancy, Charles, and Oliver), with ten-point scores by Carlos and Charles, and then in order the Little Professors, Fractions, and Brains. Susan turned in ten points for the L.P.'s, as did Linda for the Brains.

This Week's Rank	This Week's Score	Overall Score	Overall Rank
1st - Calculators	38	81	3
2nd - Fantastic Four ⎤ Tie	35	89	1
2nd - Tigers ⎦	35	73	6
4th - Math Monsters	40/32	85	2
5th - Five Alive	37/30	74	5
6th - Little Professors	26	70	8
7th - Fractions	23	78	4
8th - Brains	22	71	7

TEN-POINT SCORERS

Charlene	(Calculators	Helen	(Math Monsters)
Alfredo	(Calculators)	Luis	(Math Monsters)
Carl	(Calculators)	Carlos	(Five Alive)
Ursula	(Fantastic Four)	Charles	(Five Alive)
Rebecca	(Fantastic Four)	Susan	(Little Professors)
Lindsay	(Tigers)	Linda	(Brains)
Arthur	(Tigers)		

* * * * * *

The teams with the highest scores are recognized in a weekly one-page class newsletter. The students who exceeded their own past records by the largest amounts or who got perfect papers are also recognized in the newsletter. A typical STAD newsletter appears in Figure 2.1 (from Slavin, 1980b, p. 22). STAD is part of the Student Team Learning program at Johns Hopkins University, along with Teams-Games-Tournament and Jigsaw II (see Slavin, 1980b), and Team Assisted Individualization (Slavin, Leavey, and Madden, 1982a).

Teams-Games-Tournaments. Teams-Games-Tournaments, or TGT (DeVries and Slavin, 1978; DeVries, Slavin, Fennessey, Edwards, and Lombardo, 1980) uses the same teams, instructional format, and worksheets as STAD. However, in TGT, students play academic games to show their individual mastery of the subject matter. The game rules are illustrated in Figure 2.2 (from Slavin, 1980b, p. 28). These games are played in weekly tournaments. Students compete in the tournaments with members of other teams who are comparable in past performance. The competitions take place at tournament tables of three students. Thus a high performing student from the "Fantastic Four" might compete with a high performer from the "Pirates" and one from the "Superstars." Another table might have average performing students from the "Pirates," the "Masterminds," and the "Chiefs," and another could have low performers from the "Superstars," "Tigers," and "Masterminds." The students are not told which is the highest table, which is next, and so on, but they are told that their competition will always be fair. While teams stay together for about six weeks, the tournament table assignments are changed every week according to a system that maintains the equality of the competition. The high scorer at each table is moved to the next higher table for the next tournament, and the low scorer at each table is moved to the next lower table. This equal competition makes it possible for students of all levels of past performance to contribute maximum points to their teams if they

FIGURE 2.2   TGT Game Rules (from Slavin, 1980b, p. 28)

Reader

1.   Picks a numbered card and finds the corresponding question on the game sheet.
2.   Reads the question out loud.
3.   Tries to answer.

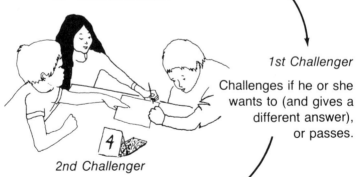

1st Challenger

Challenges if he or she wants to (and gives a different answer), or passes.

2nd Challenger

Challenges if 1st challenger passes, if he or she wants to. When all have challenged or passed, 2nd challenger checks the answer sheet. Whoever was *right* keeps the card. If the *reader* was wrong, there is no penalty, but if either challenger was wrong, he or she must put a previously won card, if any, back in the deck.

do their best, in the same way as the individual improvement score system in STAD makes it possible for everyone to be successful.

After the tournament, team scores are figured, and a newsletter is used to recognize the highest scoring teams and tournament table winners. Thus, TGT uses the same pattern of teaching, team worksheet study, individual assessment, equal opportunities for success, and team recognition as that used in STAD, but uses academic games instead of quizzes to assess learning. TGT is part of the Johns Hopkins Student Team Learning Program (Slavin, 1980b).

Team Assisted Individualization. Team Assisted Individualization (TAI) is the most recently developed of the Johns Hopkins Student Team Learning methods (Slavin, Leavey, and Madden, 1982a). It is a combination of team learning and individualized instruction applied to the teaching of mathematics. In TAI, students are assigned to 4–5 member heterogenous teams as in STAD and TGT. After being placed in the appropriate unit by means of a diagnostic test, each student works through a set of programmed mathematics units at his or her own pace. Students follow a regular sequence of activities, involving reading an instruction sheet, working on successive skillsheets that break the skill into fine subskills, taking a checkout to see if the skill has been mastered, and finally taking a test. Teammates work in pairs of their own choice, exchanging answer sheets and checking each other's skillsheets and checkouts. When a student has passed a checkout with a score of 80% or better, he or she takes a final test which is scored by a student monitor. Students' test scores and the number of tests they can complete in a week go into a team score, and team members receive certificates for exceeding preset team standards. Because of this preset standard, any number of teams can receive certificates.

Because all skillsheets and checkouts are scored by teammates and all tests are scored by student monitors, the teacher is able to work with individuals and small groups on problems they are having or to prepare them for upcoming units.

TAI is unique among all cooperative learning methods in its use of individualized instead of class-paced instruction. It was developed to be used when a class is too heterogeneous to be taught the same material at the same rate, especially when there are mainstreamed children who need the positive social interaction that takes place in the teams but also need to have material at their own level.

Jigsaw. In Aronson's (1978) Jigsaw method, students are assigned to six-member teams. Academic material is broken down into five sections. For example, a biography might be broken into early life, first accomplishments, major setbacks, later life, and world events during his or her lifetime. Each team member reads his or her unique section, except for two students who share a section (so that if one student is absent, all five topics can still be covered). Members of different teams who have studied the same sections meet in "expert groups" to discuss their sections. Then the students return to their teams and take turns teaching their teammates about their sections. Since the only way students can learn the sections other than their own is to listen carefully to their teammates, they are motivated to support and show interest in each other's work. Jigsaw does not actually use a cooperative incentive structure. Following the team reports, students may take individual quizzes covering all of the topics, and they receive individual grades on their quizzes. However, Jigsaw is classed as a cooperative learning method because it uses a cooperative task structure that creates a great deal of interdependence among students.

A modification of Jigsaw was developed by Slavin (1980b) and incorporated in the Student Team Learning program. In this method, called Jigsaw II, students work in four to five member teams as in TGT and STAD. Instead of each student having a unique section, all students read a common narrative, such as a book chapter, a short story, or a biography. However, each student is given a topic on which to become an expert. The students who had the same topics meet in expert groups to discuss them, and then return to their teams to teach what they have learned to their teammates. Then students take individual quizzes, which are formed into team scores. Improvement scores are used to form team scores, and the highest scoring teams and individuals are recognized in a class newsletter. Jigsaw II, unlike original Jigsaw, uses cooperative incentives (recognition or grades) as well as cooperative tasks.

Learning Together. The Learning Together model of cooperative learning was developed by David and Roger Johnson (1975). The cooperative methods they have researched involve students working in four to five member heterogeneous groups on assignment sheets. The groups hand in a single sheet, and receive praise as a group based on how well they are working together and how they do on the group task. In one study of Learning Together (Humphreys, Johnson, and Johnson, 1982), students received grades based on their group's average on individual achievement tests. The methods described by Johnson and Johnson (1975) include the appropriate use of competitive and individualistic methods in situations that call for them, as well as many alternative means of using cooperation. Robertson (1982) evaluated this complete program, but the program referred to in this book as "Learning Together" is the cooperative method, described above, that was used most of this research.

Group-Investigation. Group-Investigation (Sharan and Sharan, 1976), developed by Shlomo Sharan and his colleagues, is a general classroom organization plan in which students work in small groups using cooperative inquiry, group discussion, and cooperative planning and projects. In this method, students form their own two- to six-member groups. The groups choose subtopics from a unit being studied by the entire class, further break their subtopics into individual tasks, and carry out the activities necessary to prepare a group report. The group then makes a presentation or display to communicate its findings to the entire class, and is evaluated based on the quality of this report.

Other Cooperative Learning Methods. The six techniques described above are by far the most extensively researched and widely used cooperative learning methods, but there have been a few interesting studies of other methods. Wheeler (Wheeler and Ryan, 1973; Wheeler, 1977) investigated a cooperative technique in which students were assigned specific roles (such as coordinator, analyzer, or recorder) within cooperative groups and worked on social studies inquiry activities to produce a single workbook. The group making the best workbook received a prize. Peterson (Peterson and Janicki, 1979; Peterson, Janicki, and Swing, 1981) used a simple method in which students worked in four-member groups. Group members completed their own worksheets with help from their groupmates. No group rewards were given; students were simply expected to work together. Huber, Bogatzki, and Winter (1982) and Webb and Kenderski (1982) also evaluated methods involving group study but no group rewards. Starr and Schuerman (1974) used a relatively simple method in which groups of as many as eight students considered science questions and then reported back to the entire class. As in the Peterson studies, no group rewards were given. Hamblin, Hathaway, and Wodarski (1971) used a group contingency for academic performance, in which students worked in groups and earned tangible rewards (i.e., candy or toys) based on (a) the lowest three quiz scores, (b) the highest three quiz scores, or (c) the average group score. Lew and Bryant (1981) used a method somewhat similar to the Hamblin et al. low-performer contingency. They had students work in small groups, and gave the groups free time at the end of the week if *all* group members got 80% or more on a quiz. Weigel, Wiser, and Cook (1975) used a combination of cooperative methods including group information gathering, discussion, and interpretation, with prizes given to groups with the best products.

Thus, the cooperative learning methods share the idea that students work in groups to accomplish a group goal, but in every other particular they are quite different from one another. STAD, TGT, and TAI, and the Hamblin et al. and Lew and Bryant methods are highly structured, with well-specified group tasks and group rewards (recognition in a newsletter, certificates), while Group-Investigation and Learning Together give more autonomy to students and usually have less well-specified group rewards. Jigsaw and Jigsaw II are used primarily in social studies, and TAI is designed only for mathematics, while STAD, TGT, and Learning Together are used in all subjects. The original Student Team Learning methods (STAD, TGT, and Jigsaw II) use competition between teams to motivate students to cooperate within their teams, while Group-Investigation, Learning Together, TAI, and the original form of Jigsaw do not. Finally, STAD, TGT, and TAI are designed to help students learn a specific set of skills, such as adding fractions, putting commas in a series, reading charts and graphs, or understanding how chemical compounds are formed, while Group-Investigation in particular is designed primarily to get students to think creatively about concepts and learn group self-organizational skills.

3

Cooperative Learning and Student Achievement

Because cooperative learning is social, engaging, and fun, because it appears to be a humane form of classroom instruction, and because of its well-documented positive effects on a range of social outcomes (see Chapters 4–6), there are many who would advocate use of these methods whether or not they improve student achievement, as long as they do not reduce achievement. However, the primary task of schools is to provide instruction effectively. An instructional innovation that did not improve instruction would be unlikely to be used in many schools, regardless of its other effects, in an educational climate that is increasingly holding educational programs accountable for their effects on student achievement.

Most of the cooperative learning programs, especially the Student Team Learning methods, were originally developed with improving student achievement as the primary goal; only the original form of Jigsaw and the Wiegel et al. methods had a non-achievement goal (improving intergroup relations in desegregated schools) in mind at the beginning of their research.

A Typology of Cooperative Learning Methods and Student Achievement

As varied as the cooperative learning methods are, their critical features can be conceptualized in terms of two primary factors: specific group rewards based on members' learning and task specialization.

When a cooperative learning method uses *specific group rewards based on group members' learning*, this means that there is an explicit group reward based on the sum of the group members' individual learning performances, however learning is measured. For example, in the studies of the original Student Team Learning methods (STAD, TGT, Jigsaw II), high-scoring teams were recognized in a class newsletter or bulletin board. In TAI and in one of the STAD studies (Madden and Slavin, in press), students received recognition if their teams exceeded a present standard score. In the Humphreys, Johnson, and Johnson (1982) Learning Together study, students received grades based on the average of group members' scores on individual tests. In the Hamblin et al. and Lew and Bryant studies, students received rewards (tangibles or free time) based on specified score criteria. On the other side of this dimension, the methods used in the original Jigsaw, Group-Investigation, Peterson, Starr and Schuerman, Webb and Kenderski, and most of the Learning Together studies did not include formal group rewards. At most, students received praise for working in groups and to some extent for doing well as groups, but the students probably worked together more because the teacher instructed them to do so than because they were working toward a particular group goal. In the Wheeler (1977) and Wheeler and Ryan (1973) studies, group rewards were given; the groups with the best group products received prizes. However, these rewards were not based on individual group members' learning. In the Robertson (1982) Learning Together Study, student grades were primarily based on ratings of their group worksheets, but again, these group rewards were not based on the group members' individual learning.

Specific group rewards based on members' learning are hypothesized to increase the instructional effectiveness of cooperative learning methods for several reasons. Provision of specific rewards based on group performance is likely to motivate students to do whatever is necessary to make it possible for the group to succeed, because no individual can be rewarded unless the group succeeds. If mutual help, encouragement, and facilitation among group members help the group to succeed and to be rewarded, these behaviors are likely to occur when there is a group reward. However, in the particular case of learning, group rewards per se are probably not enough. It is hypothesized that *group rewards must be based on the learning of all group members* if they are to result in increased learning for all group members. The problem, discussed in Chapter 1, is that learning is a completely individual phenomenon. A group does not learn. If group success depends on a single group product, such as a single worksheet, it may be more efficient to have the one or two most able group members fill out the worksheet; in such a case, there would be little motivation for the lower-achieving students to learn the material or for the higher-achieving students to help them do so. If all students had to fill out their own worksheets, but groupmates could help one another on them, it might be more efficient for the more able students to tell their groupmates the answers than to explain the answers to them. These issues are related to the problem of diffusion of responsibility discussed in Chapter 1; unless group members are individually accountable for their own learning, their motivation to learn might be diminished by introduction of cooperative incentives and tasks.

It was hypothesized earlier that cooperative incentives increased individual performance by leading to highly contingent interpersonal sanctions favoring achievement among group members. This requires that, first, achievement of all group members does in fact contribute to group success, and, second, that the contributions of each group member can be easily seen, so that praise or blame among group members can be correctly applied. Specific group rewards based on members' learning satisfies these conditions. For this reason, it is hypothesized that specific group rewards based on group members' learning will both motivate the maximum learning efforts of all group members, and elicit encouragement, help, and facilitation among group members directed at increasing the learning of them all.

Task specialization refers to the use of techniques in which each group member is given a particular part of the group task to do, where group members depend on each other and cannot easily substitute for each other in completing the group task. For example, in the original Jigsaw method, each student in a team is given a piece of information that his or her teammates do not receive. Students depend absolutely on their groupmates to get the information they will need to do well on their own tests; more able or better prepared group members cannot cover for weaker members. Jigsaw II uses a less extreme form of specialization, where students focus on particular topics relating to a book chapter or story and are responsible for teaching their topics to their teammates. However, because all students read the same chapters or stories, teammates do not depend so absolutely on one another. In Group-Investigation, students in each group take responsibility for different parts of the group task, but the boundaries of each student's subtask are loose enough that groupmates may be able to substitute for one another to some extent. A similar form of task specialization was used by Wheeler (1977); students had individual roles in a unit on consumer research, such as surveying others to determine their preferences, testing different products, or compiling test results. A quite different kind of role assignment was used by Wheeler and Ryan (1973), where the group members were each given a role to fulfill in the group interaction, such as coordinator, analyzer, or recorder. This assignment of *roles* rather than *tasks* was not considered task specialization as all students contributed to a single group product and could easily substitute for each other.

Use of task specialization is hypothesized to increase the instructional effectiveness of cooperative learning, but only under certain circumstances. Task specialization solves the problem of diffusion of responsibility by creating a high degree of individual accountability of each group member to the group. When every group member has his or her own subtask to perform, anyone in the group can see whether (and how well) the task was done. If it is critical to the group that everyone do his or her part, task specialization will lead to interpersonal sanctions favoring effective task completion.

However, as noted earlier, learning is an outcome that has meaning only at the individual student level. As such, learning does not *inherently* lend itself to task specialization, which for learning tasks must take the form of some kind of division of responsibility. Imagine a cooperative learning method in which groups were given a broad topic to learn about, and each group member was assigned to gather information on a particular subtopic and to write a report on his or her findings. At the end of this process, the group members' reports are stapled together and handed in. This is a condition of high task specialization, because each group member must do his or her report if the group is to cover its topic; there is no problem with diffusion of responsibility. But what have the students learned? They have only been exposed to their own subtopics. If they were tested on all topics, they would fail three-quarters of the test, probably doing much worse than students who were directly taught the material.

Obviously, none of the cooperative learning methods operates in this fashion. For example, in the original form of Jigsaw, which has the highest degree of task specialization of all the cooperative learning methods, students return to their teams to teach them what they have learned about their individual topics, and all group members are ultimately tested on all the topics. The other methods that use task specialization, Jigsaw II, Group Investigation, and the Wheeler (1977) method, also have built-in opportunities for all students to learn (from each other) about all the topics, and incentives to motivate them to do so. However, only certain kinds of instructional content lend themselves to being broken into subtopics. Such content would include most of social studies and some areas of literature and science. When mastery of a specific set of skills, concepts, or facts is the instructional objective, it is difficult to break the material into subtopics and have students teach each other more effectively than would be the case in more direct instructional methods.

FIGURE 3.1 Categorization of Cooperative Learning Methods

	Specific Group Rewards Based on Members' Learning	No Specific Group Rewards or Group Rewards not Based on Members' Learning
Group Study— No Task specialization	Group Study, Group Reward for Learning STAD TGT TAI Humphreys et al. Methods Hamblin et al. Methods Lew and Bryant Methods	Group Study Learning Together Wheeler and Ryan Methods Peterson Methods Webb and Kenderski Methods Starr and Schuerman Methods Huber et al. Methods
Task Specialization	Task Specialization, Group Reward for Learning Jigsaw II	Task Specialization Jigsaw Group-Investigation Wheeler Methods

Figure 3.1 shows how the various cooperative learning methods can be categorized in terms of specific group rewards based on members' learning and task specialization. It is important to note that while group study methods are used in all subjects, task specialization is difficult to use outside of social studies or related subjects. For example, it is difficult to imagine how a mathematics lesson might be learned by having students learn unique parts of the lesson and teaching their parts to their groupmates.

Other Distinguishing Characteristics of Cooperative Learning Methods

While use or non-use of specific group rewards based on members' learning and task specialization are the most important distinguishing characteristics of the various cooperative learning methods, there are other features that vary among the methods. These include use or non-use of group competition, and use or non-use of equal opportunity scoring procedures.

Group competition is used in many cooperative learning methods to motivate students to cooperate. Because the groups with the highest scores are recognized or rewarded, students help and encourage their groupmates to achieve. The reason that group competition is used in many cooperative learning methods (especially the Student Team Learning methods) is that group recognition is the most common group incentive used in traditional classrooms. Recognition has little meaning unless there is some meaningful standard against which groups are compared, and comparison (competition) between groups is a convenient, easily understood standard. Group competition can be avoided by providing rewards (such as toys or candy) to groups based on the academic performance of their members, as was done in the Hamblin and Lew and Bryant methods, or by recognizing groups if they meet a preset standard score, as was done in the TAI studies and in the Madden and Slavin (in press) STAD study. In the Humphrey et al. (1982) and the Ziegler (1981) studies, group competition was avoided by giving the students grades based on their group's average performance, while Robertson (1982) gave students individual grades based on the quality of their group worksheets. All other methods either gave no specific group rewards at all or used group competition.

The effects of group competition on achievement should theoretically be the same as those of other methods of providing groups with specific rewards contingent on their performance, unless the competition between groups can somehow hinder group performance. For example, if two groups were put in competition with each other to build the best sand castle, and both groups had a plentiful supply of rocks with which they could destroy each other's castles, it is possible that no sand castles would be produced, because group members might find it easier to destroy the other group's sand castle than to build their own. However, it is difficult to imagine how classroom groups in competition with each other could enhance their chances of success more by hindering the learning of other groups than by doing the best possible job of learning themselves. If hindering is not a possibility, then the essential dynamics of cooperative task and incentive structures are almost identical in group competition and group non-competition, except that the standard that must be achieved for the group to be rewarded is a variable one, depending on the performance of other groups. The benefits of group competition are that if groups are fairly equal in overall potential, group competition insures each group a standard of success that is neither too difficult nor too easy to attain, and that success in a group competition is motivating to students and acceptable to a wide range of teachers.

There has been a great deal of controversy among cooperative learning researchers on the topic of group competition, with some defending its use when appropriate (Slavin, 1981a), some questioning it (Weigel, Wiser, and Cook, 1975; Johnson, 1981), and some proposing that individual student grades be based on group scores as was done in the Humphreys et al. (in press) and Ziegler (1981) studies (Deutsch, 1979; Johnson and Johnson, 1975). However, there has been little direct research on the issue of group competition vs. group non-competition. Hammond and Goldman (1961) found no differences between group competition and group non-competition on "adequacy of recommendations" in a group discussion task, although both significantly exceeded individual competition and individual non-competition treatments on this measure. Garibaldi (1979) similarly found no performance differences on a group anagram task between group competition and group non-competition. However, figuring from data presented but not analyzed in Garibaldi's paper, the group competition teams apparently performed significantly better than did non-competition teams on a Rasmussen triangle task. Julian and Perry (1967) also found higher quality group products to result from group competition than from group non-competition. Thus, the laboratory-type research favors a conclusion that group competition has a more positive effect than group non-competition on group performance, but if this is true, it is probably due to the fact that group competition can be one means of providing specific group rewards rather than to the group competition per se.

Equal opportunity scoring refers to group scoring methods used in the Student Team Learning methods, STAD, TGT, and Jigsaw II (Slavin, 1980b), and in TAI (Slavin, Leavey, and Madden, 1982). Their purpose is to give students of all levels of past performance an equal chance to contribute to their team scores if they do their best. Equal opportunity scoring takes the form of improvement scores in STAD, where the scores students contribute to their teams are based on the degree to which students' quiz scores exceed their own past averages. Use of the improvement score system is recommended for Jigsaw II (Slavin, 1980b), but the one study of Jigsaw II (Ziegler, 1981) did not use them. In TGT, competition with equals in the tournaments gives all students an equal opportunity to succeed (by winning at their tournament tables), while in TAI, the fact that students are working at their own levels means that all students have an equal chance to add to their team scores by completing units accurately at a high rate.

Equal opportunity scoring systems are hypothesized to increase student achievement for two reasons. First, it is known that when success is too easy or too difficult to achieve, motivation is low (see Atkinson, 1958; Kukla, 1972; Slavin, 1978a). In classrooms using traditional grades, high grades are too easily available to the most able students and unavailable to the least able. Because grades are strongly related to ability rather than effort, they are relatively insensitive to day-to-day or week-to-week changes in effort. Such an insensitive incentive system is unlikely to be optimal in increasing student motivation to do school work. In contrast, when improvement is the criterion for success, additional effort is likely to increase payoffs, and diminished effort is likely to decrease payoffs. The same is true of competition with equals and rewards for progress in individualized materials; increased preparation and effort are likely to lead directly and immediately to greater success. Thus, any of these methods of putting both success and failure within the reach of all students is hypothesized to increase student motivation, and thus achievement.

Second, equal opportunity scoring may be especially important in the context of cooperative learning. Cooperative learning presents the danger that because some group members are more able than others, the less able members' contributions will be devalued by their groupmates. This could remove the low achievers' motivation to try to help the group to succeed. With equal opportunity scoring, all students have an equal chance to contribute to the group score. This is hypothesized to maintain the motivation of the low achievers, thereby increasing their achievement.

In summary, the following hypotheses are advanced concerning the effects of major characteristics of cooperative learning on achievement:

1. *Specific Group Rewards Based on Members' Learning* are likely to increase the effects of cooperative learning on student achievement.
2. *Task Specialization* is likely to have a positive effect on student learning of basic skills in cooperative learning methods, but only if there are incentives for students to learn from each other and only in subjects (such as social studies) that lead themselves to being broken into subtopics.
3. *Group Competition* is likely to increase the effect of cooperative learning on student achievement, but any method of providing specific group rewards based on members' learning is likely to have the same effect.
4. *Equal Opportunity Scoring Systems* are likely to increase the effects of cooperative learning on achievement.

TABLE 3.1 Characteristics of Cooperative Learning Methods

Method	Specific Group Rewards Based on Members' Learning	Task Specialization	Group Competition	Equal-Opportunity Scoring
Group Study, Group Reward for Learning Methods				
STAD	Yes	No	Yes	Yes
TGT	Yes	No	Yes	Yes
TAI	Yes	No	No	Yes
Humphreys et al. Methods	Yes	No	No	No
Hamblin et al. Methods	Yes	No	No	No
Lew and Bryant Methods	Yes	No	No	No
Group Study Methods				
Learning Together (except Humphreys et al.)	No	No	No	No
Wheeler and Ryan Methods	No	No	Yes	No
Peterson Methods	No	No	No	No
Webb and Kenderski Methods	No	No	No	No
Starr and Schuerman Methods	No	No	No	No
Huber et al. Methods	No	No	No	No
Task Specialization, Group Reward for Learning Methods				
Jigsaw II	Yes	Yes	Yes	No
Task Specialization Methods				
Jigsaw	No	Yes	No	No
Group-Investigation	No	Yes	No	No
Wheeler Methods	No	Yes	Yes	No

Table 3.1 summarizes the characteristics of the cooperative learning methods in terms of the four dimensions discussed above. In the following sections, the evaluative research on cooperative learning methods and student achievement will be examined in light of these dimensions.

RESEARCH ON COOPERATIVE LEARNING AND ACHIEVEMENT

The effects of cooperative learning have been studied in forty-one methodologically adequate field experiments (as defined below).

Research Designs

The studies emphasized in this chapter share certain methodological characteristics. In all of them, the cooperative intervention was in place in regular elementary or secondary classrooms for at least two weeks. In all but three studies, an experiment was performed in which the cooperative groups were compared to control groups of some kind. The experimental and control groups could be assumed at the beginning of the study to be equivalent, either by means of random assignment to conditions or by use of analysis of covariance, with pretests or standardized tests as covariates; most studies used both randomization and analysis of covariance to be sure that the groups were statistically equivalent. The achievement measures used were either experimenter-made tests, in which case some procedure was followed to be sure that experimental and control groups had an equal chance to learn the material being tested, or else they were standardized tests, where neither the experimental nor control curricula were specifically keyed to the test. Experimental and control classes had the same amount of time to teach their materials. Teacher effects were partially controlled in almost all studies, either by having the same teachers teach experimental and control groups, by rotating teachers across experimental and control groups, or by randomly assigning many teachers to different groups. The three studies that did not use experiments used single-subject methods (see Herson and Barlow, 1976) capable of demonstrating cause-and-effect relationships between the cooperative treatments and increased achievement.

In the STAD, TGT, and TAI studies, teachers were usually randomly assigned to treatments from among a pool of volunteers, while in the Learning Together studies, the Wheeler studies, the Peterson studies, and some of the TGT studies, random assignment of individual students was used. Other studies used matching or other non-random methods of assignment. The forms of random assignment used are summarized in Table 3.2. Other important methodological characteristics, including sample size, grade level, study duration, location, and subject areas, are also presented in Table 3.2.

TABLE 3.2 Characteristics and Achievement Outcomes of Cooperative Learning Field Experiments

Major Reports	No. of Students	Grade Level	Duration (Weeks)	Level of Random Assignment	Kinds of Schools	Subject Areas	Achievement Effects
Student Teams-Achievement Divisions (STAD)							
Group Study, Group Reward for Learning Methods							
Slavin, 1978c	205	7	10	Class	Eastern Rural town Urban	Language Arts	0
Slavin, 1977b	62	7	10	Class	East Rural	Language Arts	+
Slavin, 1980a	424	4	12	Class	East Urban	Language Arts	+
Slavin, 1979	424	7–8	12	Class	East Rural	Language Arts	0
Slavin and Oickle, 1981	230	6–8	12	Class	East	Language Arts	+ Black Students, 0 White Students
Madden and Slavin, in press	175	3–6	6	Class	Urban East Rural	Mathematics	+
Allen and VanSickle, 1981	51	9	6	Class	South Urban	Geography	+
Slavin and Karweit, 1982	569	9	30	Teacher	East Urban	Mathematics	+
Huber, Bogatzki, and Winter, 1982	170	7	3	Class	Germany	Mathematics	+

Teams-Games-Tournament (TGT)

Study	N	Grade		Assignment	Location	Subject	
Edwards, DeVries, and Snyder, 1972	96	7	9	Class	Urban East	Mathematics	+
Edwards and DeVries, 1972	117	7	4	Student	Urban East	Mathematics	0
						Mathematics	+
Edwards and DeVries, 1974	128	7	12	Student	Urban East	Social Studies	0
Hulten and DeVries, 1976	299	7	10	Class	Urban East	Mathematics	+
DeVries, Edwards, and Wells, 1974a	191	10–12	12	Class	Suburban South	Social Studies	(+)
						Language Arts	+
DeVries and Mescon, 1975	60	3	6	Student	Suburban East	Language Arts	+
DeVries, Mescon, and Shackman, 1975a	53	3	6	Student	Suburban East	Language Arts	+
DeVries, Mescon, and Shackman, 1975b	53	3	5	Student	Suburban East	Reading	+
DeVries, Lucasse, and Shackman, 1979	1742	7–8	10	Teacher	Suburban Midwest	Language Arts	+
Combined Student Team Learning Program (STAD + TGT + Jigsaw II)							
Slavin and Karweit, 1981	559	4–5	16	Non-random (matched)	Rural East	Language Arts (STAD)	+
						Mathematics (TGT)	0
						Social Studies (Jigsaw II)	0
						Reading (STAD, Jigsaw II)	+
Team Assisted Individualization (TAI)							
Slavin, Leavey, and Madden, 1982							
Experiment 1	506	3–5	8	School	Suburban East	Mathematics	+
Experiment 2	320	4–6	10	Non-random (matched)	Suburban East	Mathematics	+

TABLE 3.2 (continued)

Major Reports	No. of Students	Grade Level	Duration (Weeks)	Level of Random Assignment	Kinds of Schools	Subject Areas	Achievement Effects
Other Group Study, Group Reward for Learning Studies							
Humphreys, Johnson, and Johnson, 1982 (Learning Together with Group Reward for Learning)	44	9	6	Student	Suburban Midwest	Science Spelling	+
Hamblin, Hathaway, and Wodarski, 1971							
Experiment 1	38	4	3	Non-Random: Latin Square	Urban Midwest	Mathematics Reading	+
Experiment 2	60	5	3	Non-Random: Latin Square	Urban Midwest	Mathematics	+
Lew and Bryant, 1981	27	4	9	Non-Random: ABABA'B Design	Suburban East	Spelling	+
Group Study Methods							
Learning Together							
Johnson, Johnson, Johnson, and Anderson, 1976	30	5	4	Student	Urban Midwest	Language Arts	0
Johnson, Johnson, & Scott, 1978	30	5–6	10	Student	Suburban Midwest	Mathematics	–
Robertson, 1982	166	2–3	6	Class	Suburban East	Mathematics	0
Other Group Study Studies							
Wheeler and Ryan, 1973	88	5–6	4	Student	Suburban Midwest	Social Studies	0
Peterson and Janicki, 1979	100	4–6	2	Student	Rural Midwest	Mathematics	0
Peterson, Janicki, and Swing, 1981	93	4–5	2	Student	Rural Midwest	Mathematics	0

Study	N	Grade		Assignment	Location	Subject	Outcome
Webb and Kenderski, 1982	107	7–8	3	Non-Random (Matched)	Urban California	Mathematics	0
Starr and Schuerman, 1974	48	7	3	Class	Suburban Midwest	Life Science	0
Huber, Bogatzki, and Winter, 1982	204	7	3	Class	Urban Germany	Mathematics	0
Task Specialization, Group Reward for Learning Methods							
Jigsaw II							
Ziegler, 1981	146	6	8	Class	Urban Canada	Social Studies	+
Task Specialization Methods							
Jigsaw							
Lucker, Rosenfield, Sikes, and Aronson, 1976	303	5–6	2	Non-Random (Matched)	Urban Southwest	Social Studies	+ Black & Hispanic Students / 0 Anglo Students
Lazarowitz, Baird, Bowlden, and Hertz-Lazarowitz, 1982	109	10–12	6	Non-Random (Matched)	Western Rural Town	Biology	0
Gonzales, 1981	182	3–4	20	Non-Random (Matched)	Rural California (Bilingual Classes)	Social Studies	0
Group Investigation							
Sharan, Ackerman, and Hertz-Lazarowitz, 1980	217	2–6	3	Non-Random (Matched)	Urban Israel	Social Studies	Gr. 2–+ 3–0 4–+ 5–0 6–+
Hertz-Lazarowitz, Sapir, and Sharan, 1981	67	8	5	Non-Random (Matched)	Urban Israel	Arabic Lang. and Culture	0
Other Task Specialization Studies							
Wheeler, 1973	88	5–6	2	Student	Southern Rural Town	Social Studies	+

Cooperative Learning and Achievement: Results

Table 3.2 summarizes the achievement outcomes of the forty-one field experiments in elementary and secondary schools that met the duration and methodological adequacy criteria described above. The achievement results are presented in the last column of the table. A "+" indicates that a statistically significant ($p<.05$) positive achievement effect was found, meaning that the cooperative learning group scored significantly higher than the control group on a test on content to which both were exposed. A "(+)" indicates a marginally significant ($p<.10$) positive effect, a "0" no differences, and a "−" a statistically significant effect favoring the control group. When significant interactions condition the meanings of main effects, the interactions are explained in the text; the entries in Table 3.2 are the main effects for the entire samples involved in the studies, unless otherwise noted.

Achievement Main Effects

Taken together, the effects of cooperative learning methods on student achievement are clearly positive. The studies summarized in Table 3.2 represent the entire universe of studies known to this author that meet the setting, duration, and methodological adequacy criteria discussed earlier in this chapter. A total of 41 studies were reviewed (Huber, Bogatzki, and Winter [1982] evaluated both STAD and a method in which students worked in groups but received no group rewards; these evaluations are presented as two separate studies). Of these, 26 (63%) showed cooperative learning methods to have some significantly positive (or, in one case, marginally positive) effect on student achievement. Fourteen (49%) found no differences, and one (2%) found significantly higher achievement for a control group than for a cooperative treatment.

However, the overall picture masks important differences between studies. Figure 3.2 illustrates these differences by breaking down the achievement results by use or non-use of specific group rewards based on members' learning and task specialization. As can be seen in the top half of Figure 3.2, there is a dramatic difference in achievement outcomes between the group study methods depending on their use of rewards. Of 25 such studies that used specific group rewards based on members' learning, 22 (88%) found positive effects on student achievement, while three (12%) found no differences. In contrast, none of the nine studies of group study methods (which did not use specific group rewards based on members' learning) found positive effects on student achievement. One (Johnson, Johnson, and Scott, 1978) found that an individualistic control group learned more than the cooperative experimental group, and the rest found no differences.

The results for task specialization are less clear. Seven of the forty-one studies used task specialization. As only one of these used task specializ-

FIGURE 3.2 Achievement Outcomes by Use or Non-Use of Specific Group Rewards Based on Members' Learning and Task Specialization

	Specific Group Rewards Based on Members' Learning			No Specific Group Rewards or Group Rewards not Based on Members' Learning			All Group Study		
Group Study— No Task Specialization	Group Study, Group Reward for Learning			Group Study			Positive	22	65%
	Positive	22	88%	Positive	0	0%	No Effect	11	32%
	No Effect	3	12%	No Effect	8	89%	Negative	1	3%
	Negative	0	0%	Negative	1	11%	N of Studies	34	
	N of Studies	25		N of Studies	9				
Task Specialization	Task Specialization, Group Reward for Learning			Task Specialization			All Task Specialization		
	Positive	1	100%	Positive	3	50%	Positive	4	57%
	No Effect	0	0%	No Effect	3	50%	No Effect	3	43%
	Negative	0	0%	Negative	0	0%	Negative	0	0%
	N of Studies	1		N of Studies	6		N of Studies	7	
	All Group Rewards for Learning Present			All Group Reward for Learning Absent			All Studies		
	Positive	23	88%	Positive	3	20%	Positive	26	63%
	No Effect	3	12%	No Effect	11	73%	No Effect	14	34%
	Negative	0	0%	Negative	1	7%	Negative	1	2%
	N of Studies	26		N of Studies	15		N of Studies	41	

ation and specific group rewards based on members' learning, there is no way to evaluate the importance of reward structure when task specialization is used. However, in this study (Ziegler, 1981), achievement effects were particularly strong, and were found to maintain on a five-month followup. Of the six studies that used task specialization without specific group rewards based on members' learning, three found positive effects on student achievement, although both the studies and the achievement effects are weaker than those characteristic of the specific group reward based on members' learning studies. Only one of the successful task specialization studies (Wheeler, 1977) used random assignment to treatments. The one successful Jigsaw study (Lucker et al., 1976) found positive effects for minority students, but not for Anglos, but these effects were not replicated by Gonzales (1981). The Sharan et al. (1980) study found positive achievement effects at the second-, fourth-, and sixth-grade levels, but only for "higher order" objectives, such as concepts, analysis of problems, and evaluation. Positive effects on lower-order objectives (e.g. knowledge, understanding, description) were found at the second-grade level only. Finally, Wheeler (1977) found greater learning under cooperative than competitive conditions for students who indicated that they preferred cooperation, but the reverse was true for students who preferred competition; however, the main effect for all students was positive. Further research on task specialization methods may resolve the issue of whether or not this is an effective form of cooperative learning for increasing student achievement, but at present the evidence supporting the effectiveness of task specialization without specific group rewards based on members' learning is weak.

Specific Group Rewards Based on Members' Learning. The evidence summarized in Table 3.2 presents unequivocal support for the observation that specific group rewards based on group members' individual learning are critical to the effectiveness of cooperative learning methods. Restricting attention to the group study methods, the presence or absence of specific group rewards based on members' learning clearly discriminates methods that increase student achievement from those that do no better than control methods. Component analyses and comparisons of similar methods further bear out the importance of this factor. Slavin (1980a) varied rewards (team vs. individual) and tasks (group vs. individual) in a study of STAD. The results of this study indicated that providing recognition based on team scores (the mean of the members' improvement scores) increased student achievement regardless of whether or not the students were allowed to study together. The students who could study in groups but received no specific group rewards learned *less* than all other students, including those who studied individually and received only individual rewards. This study also found that when students in interacting groups were working toward a team reward, they helped each other substantially more than when they could work together but received no team rewards.

Huber, Bogatzki, and Winter also compared STAD to group study without group rewards and to individual study with individual grades. They found that STAD students learned more than the individual work student, but there were no differences between the group study and individual study conditions. Finally, a study of TGT (Hulten and DeVries, 1976) found that providing recognition based on team scores (the mean of the members' game scores in the TGT tournaments) improved achievement whether or not students were permitted to study together. Group study itself had no effects on student achievement. Thus these component analyses add three more evaluations of methods that use group study but not group rewards; in no case did students in the group study conditions learn more than those in control conditions, and in one case (Slavin, 1980a) they learned less. However, in all three studies, the addition of specific group rewards based on members' learning made the methods instructionally effective.

The importance of specific group rewards based on members' learning is also clearly demonstrated in a comparison of the four Learning Together studies. Johnson, Johnson, Johnson, and Anderson (1976), Johnson, Johnson, and Scott (1978) and Robertson (1982) evaluated a group study method in which students worked in small groups to complete a single group worksheet. The groups were "praised and rewarded" for working together, but there was no way for group members to see exactly how much each student learned or contributed to the group worksheet. In fact, individual student *learning* was inconsequential for the groups to be rewarded. The Johnson, Johnson, and Scott (1978) study was the only cooperative learning study to find greater learning for a control group than for the cooperative learning group, and there were no experimental-control differences found in the Johnson, Johnson, Johnson, and Anderson (1976) and Robertson(1982) studies.

In contrast, Humphreys, Johnson, and Johnson (1982) evaluated an experimental treatment that was identical to the one used in the earlier Learning Together research in every respect but one; instead of being praised and rewarded as a group for completing a single worksheet, students studied together but took individual quizzes. They then received grades based on the *average* of their group's quizzes. Students in this treatment learned significantly more than students in an individualistic control group similar to the control groups used in the earlier Learning Together studies. Since the use of grades based on the average group members' learning is the only feature distinguishing the Humphreys et al. method from the other Learning Together methods, it can be inferred that it was the specific group rewards based on members' learning that made the difference.

Research at the college level on peer-monitoring methods provided important further substantiation of the critical role played by specific group rewards based on members' learning in the effectiveness of cooperative learning for increasing student learning. Two related articles (Beaman, Diener, Frazer, and Endresen, 1977; Fraser, Beaman, Diener, and Kelem,

1977) summarized the results of five studies of peer-monitoring conducted in psychology classes at the University of Washington. In all of these studies, students were assigned a partner (in one case one, two, or three partners) with whom to study course materials outside of class. In three of the studies, experimental students received grades based on the average of the test scores they and their partner(s) earned, while control students had no partners and received individual grades only. Two of these studies found substantial and statistically significant differences in performance favoring the peer-monitoring groups over the control groups, while the third found marginally significant differences ($p<.08$) in the same direction. In the remaining two studies, students studied in groups but received individual grades only. While marginally significant differences ($p<.10$) favoring the peer-study group were found in one of the studies that did not use grade averaging, the other found no differences. Other cooperative learning studies at the college level that have not used specific group rewards based on members' learning have tended to find that the students in the cooperative classes learned no more than did students in traditional lecture classes (McClintock and Sonquist, 1976; Gnagney, 1962) and in some cases learned less (Young, 1971).

The pattern of results, both across the different methods and within the component analyses, support an unexpected conclusion: the opportunity for students to study together makes little or no contribution to the effects of cooperative learning on achievement. Simply telling students to work together has never been found (among the studies that meet the criteria for inclusion applied in this book) to increase student achievement more than telling them to work separately. In two cases (Johnson, Johnson, and Scott, 1978; Slavin, 1980a) allowing students to work together without giving them a group goal or making them dependent on one another's achievement in some other way resulted in *lower* achievement than was seen in conditions in which students worked alone. On the other hand, studies of group study methods in which cooperative learning students could earn group rewards based on group members' academic performance were relatively consistent in showing the superiority of these methods to individualistic, competitive, or traditional control methods. There is some suggestion that specific group rewards based on members' learning increase student achievement even in the absence of group interaction (Hulten and DeVries, 1976; Slavin, 1980a).

Task Specialization. As noted above, four of the seven studies of methods using task specialization (the provision of unique subtasks to each group member) found positive effects on student achievement. However, while inconsistencies and interactions in the successful studies, as well as the small number of studies in which task specialization was used, make definite conclusions difficult to draw, these findings suggest that methods using task specialization may be effective in increasing student achievement, whether or not specific group rewards based on members' learning are used.

All four of the successful studies of methods that used task specialization took place in social studies. The comparisons that did not find positive achievement effects for cooperative learning methods that use task specialization were the evaluations of Group-Investigation by Hertz-Lazarowitz, Sapir, and Sharan (1981) in Arabic language and culture classes, and studies of Jigsaw by Lazarowitz et al. (1982) in high school biology classes and by Gonzales (1981) in social studies. As noted earlier, social studies units lend themselves to being broken into subtopics (Jigsaw and Jigsaw II) or subtasks in action-oriented projects (Group-Investigation and the Wheeler (1977) method). In the study by Hertz-Lazarowitz and her colleagues (1981), the authors noted that using Group-Investigation to teach Arabic might not have been an optimal use of the method, because students only focused on part of the entire subject matter in their groups.

The differences in task specialization between the two otherwise quite similar Wheeler studies illustrates the importance of this variable, Wheeler (1977) assigned cooperative groups the task of producing a single workbook. Each student was given a specific role in a problem-solving unit on consumer research involving determining which brand of plastic wrap was the best buy for a certain use. For example, one student surveyed others to determine their brand preferences, another tested different brands to determine relative strengths, a third compiled test results in the group's workbook, and so on. This was considered a case of task interdependence, because each student had a unique task, and others could not substitute for a student who failed to perform his or her task. Students who worked in these cooperative groups learned significantly more about the problem-solving process as it related to consumer research than did students who were responsible for all tasks and were in individual competition to make the best workbook.

In contrast, Wheeler and Ryan (1973) used an almost identical design but failed to find differences between a cooperative condition and a competitive one. In this study, students were given individual *roles*, but not individual *tasks*, in preparing a workbook for a unit on "adaptation" among the Iban of Borneo and the Eskimo of Alaska. The roles included "coordinator," "analyzer," "recorder," and so on. Although each student had his or her own role, students could substitute for one another in the various activities leading up to preparing the final workbooks. For this reason, the Wheeler and Ryan (1973) study was not considered a case of task specialization. Even though the Wheeler and Ryan (1973) study was identical to the Wheeler (1977) study in most respects, this difference in task specialization may have led to the finding of no achievement differences between the cooperative and competitive conditions in the earlier study. The Wheeler (1977) method that used task specialization was high in individual accountability, because students depended on one another to do their parts, while the Wheeler and Ryan (1973) method was low in individual accountability, because more able or hardworking students could do the entire task.

One Group-Investigation study (Sharan, Hertz-Lazarowitz, and Ackerman, 1980) provides an insight into the kinds of educational objectives best achieved under different forms of cooperative learning. In that study, two kinds of questions were used: questions requiring "higher-order cognition" (identifying concepts, analysis of problems, judgment, evaluation, and imagination) and those requiring "low-level thinking" (memory, information, understanding, description, and establishing the sequence of events). Significant differences favoring the Group-Investigation classes were found at three of the five grade levels studied for the "higher-order" questions, but at only one of the five for "low-level" questions. These differences in the number of significant effects are hardly large enough to be conclusive, but it is interesting to note that the Group-Investigation treatment, which uses task specialization and a high degree of student autonomy, was apparently most successful in affecting the kind of concepts that would be least specific to any particular subtask (e.g., judgment, evaluation, imagination) and least successful with concepts that would be likely to be the most specific to each subtask (e.g., information, description). In other words, it may be that students in methods involving task specialization are primarily learning ways to approach social studies questions (which might be common to all subtasks) rather than specific information or skills relating to the social studies unit. Similarly, in the Wheeler (1977) study, students were clearly being tested on how to approach problems like the consumer testing of plastic wrap (experienced in different ways in all subtasks), not on details of the testing procedures or results (which would be particular to each subtask). In Jigsaw and Jigsaw II, there is a specific peer teaching activity after students work on their own subtopics, so there is less dependence on concepts that cross-cut the subtopics; however, it may be that the effects of Jigsaw and Jigsaw II are also strongest for higher-order concepts that could be learned in studying each subtopic.

In summary, task specialization appears to increase the effectiveness of cooperative learning in certain areas of social studies. The evidence collected so far is scanty, but it seems to indicate that methods using task specialization are most likely to be effective for teaching high-order concepts.

Group Competition. Methods that use group competition are somewhat more likely than those that do not to produce positive achievement effects. Of 20 studies in which group competition was used, 16 (80%) found positive achievement effects. Ten (48%) of the 21 studies not using group competition found positive effects on student achievement, ten (48%) found no differences, and one (5%) found greater learning in the control group. A more detailed consideration of the studies that do and do not use group competition suggests that use of group competition increases the effectiveness of cooperative learning methods only as one among many ways to provide groups with rewards based on their members' learning. Eight of the ten successful studies of methods that did not involve group competition did provide specific group rewards based on members' achievement. The one STAD study that did not use group competition (Madden and Slavin, in press) gave the teams recognition for exceeding a preset average score. In the TAI studies (Slavin, Leavey, and Madden, 1982), teams were given certificates for exceeding set standards, in this case based on the number and accuracy of all units completed by all team members. The Humphreys, Johnson, and Johnson (1982) study of Learning Together and the Ziegler (1981) Jigsaw II study gave students grades based on their group's average on individually administered tests. In the two Hamblin et al. (1971) studies and the Lew and Bryant (1981) study, groups received tangible rewards based on their members' learning. The other two successful non-competition studies, one of the Group-Investigation studies (Sharan, Ackerman, and Hertz-Lazarowitz, 1980) and the Jigsaw study (Lucker, Rosenfield, Sikes, and Aronson, 1976), both used task specialization to motivate students to encourage their groupmates. Use of group competition by Wheeler and Ryan (1977) did not result in improved achievement, probably because the competition was based on ratings of a workbook produced by the group rather than a sum of individual performances or a product of performance of distinct subtasks.

One of the TGT studies (Edwards and DeVries, 1974) compared TGT with group competition to TGT without group competition. In the group competition condition, the highest scoring teams were recognized in a weekly class newsletter. In the non-competition treatment, each team received its own newsletter, listing the team members' scores and comparing the team's score to the maximum it could have achieved. Mathematics achievement was significantly higher in the group-competition treatment than in the group non-competition treatment. However, note that in the group non-competition treatment, no group rewards were given at all. Since the teams had no basis of comparison, their team scores were meaningless, except that they could compare each week's score to the team's own past record. In other words, this non-competition treatment also did not use a specific group reward based on members' learning, and it is probably for this reason, not because of the non-competition itself, that lower achievement was seen. In contrast, the one STAD study that did not use group competition (Madden and Slavin, in press) did use team recognition based on preset standards, and in this case the failure to use group competition did not diminish the effectiveness of STAD for student achievement. Thus group competition apparently has a positive effect on student achievement only in so far as it serves as a means of providing specific group rewards based on members' learning, but non-competitive means of providing such reward are equally effective.

Equal Opportunity Scoring. Team scores based on individual improvement scores (STAD and Jigsaw II), competition with equals (TGT), or progress through individualized materials (TAI) are used only in the Student Team Learning methods, so the effects of this component cannot be separated from the effects of Student Team Learning as a complete program. Taking the STAD, TGT, Jigsaw II, and TAI studies together, there are twenty-two studies, of which 19 (86%) found positive results. This percentage is higher than that for non-STL studies; seven (37%) of nineteen non-STL studies had positive findings. However, there is no evidence that Student Team Learning methods are more effective than other methods that use specific group rewards based on members' learning.

Studies specifically evaluating "equal opportunity for success" scoring systems have provided some support for the effectiveness of this component. Slavin (1980c) evaluated the improvement score system used in STAD and found that rewarding students based on the degree to which their quiz scores exceeded their own past averages significantly increased their achievement. One replication of that study (Beady, Slavin, and Fennessey, 1981) found achievement to be higher, but not significantly higher, in the improvement score condition, and a second replication (Beady and Slavin, 1981) found a significant positive effect for blacks but not for whites. Slavin (1978) evaluated a comparison-with-equals scoring system in which students were rewarded based on the rank of their quiz score among an ability-homogeneous "achievement division." This treatment had no statistically significant effects on student achievement, but it did significantly increase student time on-task. On balance, there does appear to be some indication of a positive effect of equal opportunity scoring on student achievement, but the evidence at this point is by no means clear in support of this.

Setting and Design Differences between Studies. In addition to the substantive differences discussed above, setting and design differences between studies may explain some differences in achievement outcomes. Table 3.3 summarizes the outcomes of the cooperative learning studies broken down by important methodological characteristics.

As is apparent in Table 3.3, grade level has little bearing on study outcomes; positive effects were only slightly more likely to be found at the elementary (2–6) level than at the secondary (6–12) level. Study duration (longer or shorter than seven weeks) and study sample size (less than the median (117) or greater than or equal to the median) each had a small effect on study outcomes. Longer and larger studies were slightly more likely than shorter or smaller ones to find positive effects. Also, studies that used random assignment of classes, teachers, or schools, or single-subject designs, were somewhat more likely than those using matching or random assignment of students to find positive achievement effects.

However, these methodological differences do not affect the substantive conclusions. For example, all ten smaller-than-median group study,

TABLE 3.3   Summary of Effects of Cooperative Learning on Achievement Broken Down by Setting and Design Characteristics

| | Effects on Achievement | | | Number |
	Positive	No Effect	Negative	of Studies
All Studies	26 (63%)	14 (34%)	1 (2%)	41
Elementary (2–6)	15 (68%)	6 (27%)	1 (5%)	22
Secondary (6–12)	11 (58%)	8 (42%)	0 (0%)	19
Shorter than 7 weeks	12 (52%)	11 (48%)	0 (0%)	23
Longer than 7 weeks	14 (78%)	3 (17%)	1 (6%)	18
Sample size < 117	11 (55%)	8 (40%)	1 (5%)	20
Sample size ≥ 117	15 (71%)	6 (29%)	0 (0%)	21
Random Assignment of Students	6 (50%)	5 (42%)	1 (8%)	12
Random Assignment of Classes/Teachers/Schools	13 (72%)	5 (28%)	0 (0%)	18
Non-Random Assignment (Matching)	4 (50%)	4 (50%)	0 (0%)	8
Single-Subject Designs	3 (100%)	0 (0%)	0 (0%)	3

group reward for learning studies found positive effects on student achievement, while none of the seven smaller-than-median group study studies found such effects. Nine of the ten shorter-than-median group study, group reward for learning studies found positive achievement effects, but none of the eight shorter-than-median group study studies found positive effects.

Cooperative Learning and Achievement: Conclusions

The results of the field experimental research on cooperative learning supports the following conclusions:

1. Cooperative learning methods that use specific group rewards based on group members' individual learning consistently increase achievement more than control methods.
2. Cooperative learning methods that use task specialization may increase student achievement more than control methods, but at present the data are inconclusive and the positive results are limited to certain areas of social studies or related subjects.
3. Cooperative learning methods that use group study but neither specific group rewards based on members' learning nor task specialization do not increase student achievement more than control methods.
4. Group competition increases the instructional effectiveness of cooperative learning, but only as one among many ways of providing specific group rewards based on members' learning.
5. Equal opportunity scoring procedures may have a positive effect on student achievement, but this is unclear at present.

Cooperative Incentives vs. Cooperative Tasks. The most striking conclusion from cooperative learning research is that among methods that do not use task specialization, it is the *cooperative incentive structure* that explains the effectiveness of the cooperative learning methods; there is no evidence that task structure (group study) makes any difference in student achievement. Perhaps this should not be surprising. The theory on which cooperative learning is based is a theory of *incentive* structures, not of *task* structures. Almost all of the early laboratory studies on cooperation involved giving money, prizes, or grades to individuals operating under various sets of cooperative, competitive, or individualistic rules. Deutsch's (1949b) theory of cooperation and competition clearly assumes that the performance outcomes of these incentive systems depend on the relationship between others' behaviors and one's own *rewards*. Later theoretical statements (e.g., Johnson and Johnson, 1974; Slavin, 1977a) also focus on the *reward* consequences of actions taken to help or hinder others in cooperative, competitive, and individualistic incentive systems. Task interdependence (Miller and Hamblin, 1963) and type of task (Johnson and Johnson, 1974; Slavin, 1977a) have been considered as conditioning or enabling components of a cooperative reward structure. But a theory of task structures that would support an expectation that individuals working together without cooperative goals would perform or learn better than individuals working separately has never been formulated. Thus it should not come as a surprise that the cooperative learning research does not find that students working in small groups learn better, unless the group members are given clear incentives for doing well as a group. Group tasks would seem particularly unlikely to increase individual student *learning* (as opposed to other performance outcomes). In the typical classroom, there is little reason for students to care whether or not their classmates are learning. Students may help each other get through worksheets or solve problems, because it is likely that if two or more students pool their efforts, they can finish a worksheet or problem more quickly and accurately than they can working alone, and in fact the research on small group learning without clear group incentives does consistently show that worksheets or problems are completed more quickly and accurately in groups than by individuals (Johnson, Johnson, Johnson, and Anderson, 1976; Johnson, Johnson, and Scott, 1978; Johnson, Johnson, and Skon, 1970; Johnson and Johnson, 1979). However, as noted previously, finishing a worksheet quickly or accurately in a group setting has little meaning for the individual learning of the group members. In a learning group simply given the task of finishing worksheets together, there is little reason for students to make sure that their groupmates are learning. In fact, the most efficient strategy is probably to poll group members to get consensus on the best answer to each question. If someone wants an explanation of a particular answer, it is inefficient to give it to him or her, as the explanation does not serve anyone's purposes (probably including the student who did not understand) and slows down the group. There is evidence that students believe that the purpose of seatwork is to finish it, not to learn from it (Anderson, 1981), so to ask that students perceive their classmates' learning of material on worksheets as an important goal (let alone their own learning) is asking a great deal.

There are several ways in which specific rewards for group output might increase student achievement in cooperative learning, and all of them probably operate to some degree. The most obvious effect is to get students to care about the academic performance of their peers, by making each student's rewards depend in part on the academic achievement of the student's peers. This interdependence for reward is likely to motivate students to help one another. In this case, the "help" students provide each other is likely to focus on *learning*, not on simply getting through a set of materials, because it is the sum of group members' scores on individual assessments of knowledge that brings rewards to the group in all of the methods that use specific group rewards based on members' learning. If a group finishes its worksheets without making sure that all group members understand the content, the group will fail.

The observation that specific group rewards based on members' learning increase student achievement by activating effective helping behaviors is supported by the Hamblin, Hathaway, and Wodarski (1971) studies. In the first of these experiments, students worked in groups of about nine members under each of five contingencies: rewards based on the *lowest three* quiz scores, the *highest three* scores, the *average* of the members' scores, *individual performance*, or *individual attendance* (i.e., not contingent on performance). Performance in three different subjects was highest in the low three and high three contingencies. More importantly, the three most able students in each group learned best in the high three contingency, while the three least able learned best in the low three contingency. Apparently, when the group's rewards were contingent on improving the learning of one category of students, the group was able to do so effectively. In the second Hamblin et al. (1971) experiment, it was found that the frequency of peer tutoring and actual student achievement increased in a linear fashion as the proportion of student's rewards dependent on the lowest three scores in their groups increased from zero to 33% to 67% to 100%. These results suggest that effective tutoring is activated by the provision of rewards to the group based on group members' achievement.

However, focusing helping on the individual learning of group members is only one likely effect of specific group rewards. Group rewards are also likely to motivate students to encourage one another to learn. As soon as students realize that they must not only do well themselves, but must somehow induce their groupmates to achieve, they are likely to apply interpersonal sanctions in favor of doing well academically. In several of the Student Team Learning studies, students in STAD and TGT classes have indicated much more agreement with such statements as "other children in my class want me to work hard" than have control students (see Slavin, 1981b). Students' perceptions that their classmates want them to excel probably have a strong effect on their own motivations to do so, and contrast sharply with the situation in classrooms in which individual competition for grades leads students to express peer norms *against* academic excellence (see Coleman, 1961; Slavin, 1981b). Peer sanctions for or against academic striving may be stronger in many cases than teacher or parent pressure to achieve, especially for adolescents and for lower-class students (see Spilerman, 1971). In such cases, changing peer norms to favor academic efforts may be especially important.

However, there are less obvious impacts of peer sanctions favoring academic achievement. The traditional grading system is theoretically deficient for three primary reasons (see Slavin, 1978a). One is that its competitive nature leads students to express norms against academic excellence to attempt to lower the standards against which they will be evaluated. Another is that grades are delivered so infrequently, and on such a complex basis, that it is difficult for a student to see the connection between an increase in effort today and a grade in several weeks. The third deficiency is that good grades are too easily available to some students and impossibly difficult to attain for others, conditions posited by Atkinson (1958) and Kukla (1972) to create minimal motivation.

When students are operating under a cooperative incentive structure with specific rewards for group performance, they are likely to establish an interpersonal incentive structure of their own, in which students' academic efforts are praised by their peers (see Slavin, 1981b). This interpersonal incentive system is likely to be quite sensitive and contingent on students' efforts. Interpersonal praise is likely to be delivered close in time to the performance of the desired behaviors, at least to the degree that students' performances are quantifiable and visible to their groupmates (see the discussion of individual accountability below). Students may feel that they can get shoddy work past their teachers, but not their peers, the way a musician might feel he or she could get by with a less than perfect performance in the orchestra that would be immediately noticed in an individual music lesson. It may be as much the highly contingent nature of peer sanctions for academic achievement as the fact that it comes from a peer that makes peer support for academic achievement effective.

Finally, specific rewards based on group output may increase student achievement by altering the situation in which academic success is guaranteed to some (high-ability students) and barred to others (low-ability students). In the Student Team Learning programs, this problem is directly addressed by an emphasis on improvement scores (STAD and Jigsaw II), competition with equals (TGT), or individualized materials (TAI). However, the fact of putting students on a team (even in the absence of equal opportunity scoring) attenuates the problem of unequal access to academic rewards. Low-ability students who work especially hard may not improve their chances of getting "A's," but they may well improve their group's chances of being successful. Similarly, high-ability students who do more than the minimum required for an "A" will increase their groups' chances of success. Even though the grading system may still be insensitive to the extra efforts of these low- and high-ability students, their groupmates are likely to appreciate their efforts.

Figure 3.3 depicts a theoretical model of the effects on learning of specific group rewards based on members' learning. It is interesting to compare this model to Figure 1.1 in Chapter 1. As group member support for performance was central to the model linking cooperative incentives and tasks to performance in general, peer norms and sanctions supporting learning are critical in linking group rewards based on members' learning to student motivation, and thereby to increased learning. Two elements of Figure 3.3 did not appear in Figure 1.1: attenuation of unequal opportunities for success, and sensitive, contingent interpersonal incentives for learning. These elements are important only in the school setting, where the traditional incentive system is hypothesized to be deficient in that it gives students unequal opportunities for success and is insensitive to changes in student effort on performance, elements that are not characteristic of the control groups in the laboratory-type studies on which Figure 1.1 was based. Diffusion of responsibility, an important part of Figure 1.1, is diminished by the sensitive, contingent interpersonal incentives for individual learning administered by groupmates. In cooperative learning techniques in which specific group rewards are given based on

FIGURE 3.3   Theoretical Model of Effects on Learning of Specific Group Rewards Based on Members' Learning

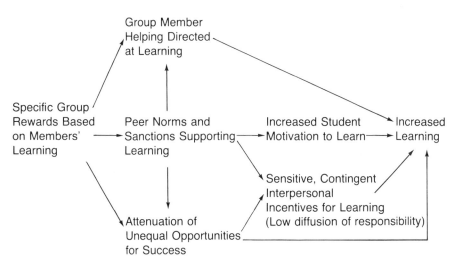

members' learning, a group reward is usually based on a sum or average of the members' performance on a learning measure. If group members are made aware of each other's scores, there is little opportunity for diffusion of responsibility, as group members can hold each other accountable for their scores. If the individuals' scores were secret, some diffusion of responsibility would be possible, but group members would still want to assess each other's learning to be sure that everyone was going to do well on the upcoming individual assessment. This within-group checking would of course reduce diffusion of responsibility. See the section later in this chapter on individual accountability for more on this topic.

It should be noted that not all of the paths illustrated in Figure 3.3 have direct empirical support. It is known that group rewards based on members' learning produce peer norms favoring learning (Slavin, 1981b), and there is substantial evidence outside of the cooperative learning literature that peer norms favoring achievement are associated with high achievement, controlling for student background (see Brookover, Beady, Flood, Schweitzer, and Wisenbacker, 1979; Coleman, 1961). Group rewards do appear to increase group member helping (Hamblin et al., 1971; Slavin, 1980a), and there is some evidence to suggest that helping in the context of specific group rewards based on members' learning (when it focuses clearly on learning outcomes) improves achievement (Hamblin, et al., 1971). It is apparently true that for most academic tasks, helping that is *not* done in the context of a specific group reward based on members' learning does *not* increase student achievement. However, while it seems logical that helping focused on learning outcomes in the context of group rewards for members' learning would increase achievement, the findings of the Hulten and DeVries (1976) and Slavin (1980a) studies suggest that the effects of cooperative learning on achievement may be most strongly mediated by motivational factors, which are primarily influenced by the changes in peer norms and sanctions concerning achievement brought about by the cooperative incentive structure.

Task Specialization. The evidence at present concerning the effects of task specialization on student achievement is too unclear to justify firm conclusions. If further research on cooperative learning methods that use task specialization finds positive achievement effects, the explanation for these effects would focus on two issues. One is individual accountability. Task specialization creates very high levels of individual accountability, as each group member's task can be easily seen and evaluated by his or her groupmates, and the quality of the task is critical to the group. Thus, motivation for each group member to perform his or her own task well is probably quite high. If the learning objective is so general or diffuse that it allows each student to learn something different, then learning should be enhanced by task specialization. This may explain the positive effects of Group-Investigation on "higher-level" skills, which tend to be common to many specific topics, as opposed to "lower-level skills" which are more particular to the content studied.

The second issue important in explaining effects of task specialization on achievement depends on mechanisms to insure that students are motivated and able to learn each others' topics. For example, in Jigsaw, students are individually tested on all of the topics, and they receive individual grades based on their test scores. Even though this individual grading is an individual or competitive incentive structure, not a cooperative one, it drives the cooperative activity within the groups, as it makes students depend on one another for information they will need to do well as individuals. Without a strong motivation to learn each others' topics, students in task specialization methods are unlikely to learn more than in traditional classrooms. However, more evidence is needed on task specialization methods before we can understand how they might affect student achievement.

Group Rewards and Individual Accountability. The lessons learned from the field experimental research on cooperative learning methods and student achievement can be reduced to a single principle: learning is enhanced by provision of group rewards if and only if group members are individually accountable to the group for their own learning. Individual accountability can be created either by providing specific group rewards based on members' learning, or by having students perform unique tasks and providing incentives for students to learn from each other. Of thirty-two cooperative learning studies that used either specific group rewards based on members' learning or task specialization, positive effects on student achievement were found in 26 (81%); none of the nine studies that used neither specific group rewards based on members' learning nor task specialization found such effects. A combination of group rewards and individual accountability creates interdependence among group members based on each other's learning, which activates all of the mechanisms hypothesized to lead to higher achievement summarized in Figure 3.3: helping among groupmates, peer norms and sanctions favoring achievement, and attenuation of unequal opportunities for success. Only if group rewards depend on the learning of each group member are group members likely to establish the interpersonal sanctions favoring learning that motivate students to learn because their peers want them to do so. Individual accountability solves the problem of diffusion of responsibility, discussed in Chapter 1. In cooperative learning methods that are low in individual accountability, any group member can theoretically do all of the group's work, and it is possible the group could be successful if it had a single bright or hard-working student. In such methods, there is no way for group members to be able to say with any certainty how much each of them contributed to the group. In other words, when individual accountability is low, the possibility that diffusion of responsibility will take place is high, as the connection between each individual's efforts and the group's success is unclear.

COOPERATIVE LEARNING AND ACHIEVEMENT: INTERACTIONS

Ability X Treatment Interactions.   The evidence for ability X treatment interactions in cooperative learning is quite mixed. In some cases, when no ability X pretest interactions have been found, this fact has not been reported, as a non-finding for an interaction is usually of little interest. In cooperative learning studies in which ability X treatment interactions have been found, they are as likely to show disproportionate effects favoring high achievers as low achievers. One TGT study (Hulten and DeVries, 1976) found ability X treatment interactions favoring high achievers in TGT classes, while two different TGT studies (DeVries, Mescon, and Shackman, 1975a; Edwards, DeVries, and Snyder, 1972) found that low achievers gained the most in TGT. Four TGT studies found no ability X treatment interactions (DeVries and Mescon, 1975; DeVries, Mescon, and Shackman, 1975b; Edwards and DeVries, 1972, 1974). Three STAD studies (Slavin, 1977b; Slavin and Karweit, 1982; Slavin and Oickle, 1981) found interactions favoring low achievers in the STAD classes. However, these interactions were more likely to have been artifacts of race X treatment interactions than true ability X treatment interactions (see below). One of the TAI studies (Slavin, Leavey, and Madden, 1982) found an interaction, showing disproportionate positive effects on low achievers, but because the combination of teams and individualized instruction used in TAI was specifically developed to incorporate low achievers, this should not be taken as an effect of teams per se. On the other hand, the second TAI study (Slavin, Leavey, and Madden, 1982) found no interactions between ability and treatment.

A few of the cooperative learning studies were specifically designed to study aptitude X treatment interactions. One (Peterson and Janicki, 1979) found a marginally significant ability X treatment interaction favoring high achievers in a small group treatment on a delayed posttest, but not on an immediate posttest. Webb and Kenderski (1982) found a similar interaction favoring high achievers in the small group treatment. However, Peterson, Janicki, and Swing (1981) used quite similar methods and found a curvilinear interaction on immediate as well as delayed posttests, where high and low achievers learned best in a small group treatment while average achievers learned best working independently. This last finding was further supported by a shorter laboratory-type study (Webb, 1977) in which a curvilinear pattern was also found. The same Webb (1977) study also found that while high and low achievers gained the most in mixed-ability groups, this curvilinear effect was not found in homogeneous middle-ability groups. Webb (in press a) replicated this difference between the different kinds of groups. These findings may explain the inconsistent interactions seen in other studies; it may be that cooperative learning is best for high and low achievers (as opposed to average achievers), and that characteristics of the samples or measures in various studies bring out the effects for one but not the other extreme group (high or low achievers). Also, because curvilinear trends have only been tested in the Peterson and Webb studies, it may be that these did in fact exist in other studies, but they were undetected. However, this is pure speculation at this point. The Peterson and Webb findings are themselves inconsistent, and interactions (especially curvilinear ones) are notoriously difficult to replicate and interpret. More research along the lines of these studies will be needed to resolve this issue.

Race X Treatment Interactions. While interactions between ability and treatment have been inconsistent in direction in the cooperative learning studies, race X treatment interactions, when found, have consistently supported the observation that blacks (and possibly Chicanos as well) gain outstandingly in cooperative learning. A race X treatment interaction of this kind was found in two STAD studies (Slavin, 1977b; Slavin and Oickle, 1981), and in one Jigsaw study (Lucker, Rosenfield, Sikes, and Aronson, 1976), in which blacks and Chicanos were analyzed together as "minorities." A third STAD study (Slavin, 1979) failed to find this interaction, but a race X treatment interaction favoring black achievement was found in an evaluation of the improvement score system used in STAD (Beady and Slavin, 1981).

The race X treatment interactions found in the Slavin and Oickle (1981) study were analyzed in some detail to determine whether they were an artifact of an ability X treatment interaction, or represent a true race X treatment effect. It was impossible to clearly separate these possibilities, as the correlation between race and pretest score was 0.43 (with blacks scoring lower). Interestingly, while there were significant pretest achievement differences between blacks and whites in the experimental and control groups, these differences disappeared on the posttests for the STAD group, while they remained in the control group. There were no pretest X treatment interactions within race groups. The pattern of results supported a conclusion that while pretest X treatment interactions may have made a contribution to the race X treatment interaction, there was also a true race X treatment effect not explained away by pretest differences between blacks and whites. This conclusion is buttressed by the observation that while all of the race X treatment interactions have shown disproportionate gains for blacks, ability X treatment interactions have been inconsistently observed and inconsistent in direction. Of the four studies discussed above that found significant ability X treatment interactions showing disproportionately positive effects for low achievers, two are STAD studies in which stronger race X treatment interactions were observed (Slavin, 1977b; Slavin and Oickle, 1981), and a third (Edwards,

DeVries, and Snyder, 1972) took place in integrated classrooms (although race X treatment interactions were not computed).

If the race X treatment interactions observed in the studies cited above are not artifacts, it is important to explain them. One possible explanation is that there is something in black and Hispanic psychology or culture that makes cooperation in more effective motivational system than competition for minority students. There is some evidence to support this possibility. For blacks, the peer group is usually of greater importance than it is for whites. Black children's self-esteem depends more on how they see themselves getting along with their peer group than how they are doing academically, while the reverse is true for whites (Hare, 1977). When given a choice to compete or cooperate with a peer, blacks (DeVoe, 1977; Richmond and Weiner, 1973) and Mexican-Americans (Kagan and Madsen, 1971) are more likely than Anglos to cooperate. Wheeler (1977) found that students who tended to choose cooperation over competition learned best in a cooperative learning method, while students who chose to compete learned best under competition. If blacks and Mexican-Americans are more predisposed to cooperate, then they may simply learn best in an instructional method that matches their predisposition.

In the traditional American classroom, students are in competition with one another for a limited supply of good grades and other rewards. Serious competition disrupts interpersonal bonds (see Johnson and Johnson, 1974). Many students are caught in a bind: to attempt to excel academically and risk alienating their peers, or to do the minimum needed to get by. Students who have more allegiance to their peer group than to a goal of academic success may choose the latter.

Cooperative learning methods tend to make learning a peer-supported activity, because doing well benefits peers rather than making them look bad. Three studies (Hulten and DeVries, 1976; Madden and Slavin, in press; Slavin, 1978c) have found that cooperative learning changes peer norms to favor learning, and two additional studies have shown that students in cooperative learning classes who were academically successful relative to their own past performances gained in sociometric status (i.e., the number of their peers who chose them as friends increased), while control students who were academically successful lost status (Slavin, DeVries, and Hulten, 1975; Slavin, 1975). Changing achieving academically from a peer-opposed activity to a peer-supported one is likely to have the greatest effect on the most peer-oriented students.

Obviously, more research will be needed both to establish the existence of race X treatment interactions on achievement and to explain them. This issue could have importance beyond cooperative learning. While it is premature to make any conclusions, it may ultimately be found that the differences in achievement between Anglo and minority students are due in part to differences in peer support for achievement in the different ethnic groups, and that if peer support for achievement can be altered, the minority–Anglo achievement gap can be diminished.

Process-Product Studies of Small Group Learning

The studies cited earlier in this chapter have focused on *outcomes* of cooperative learning. However, recent research on the processes by which students learn in small groups has begun to shed light on the particular behaviors associated with achievement gain in small group learning. This research is modeled on process-product research (see, for example, Brophy, 1979). Students working in groups are carefully observed, and then they are tested on whatever the group was studying. Correlations are computed between the frequencies of each of several behaviors and achievement, usually controlling for ability or pretest. This research has been reviewed recently by Webb (in press b), so only a brief summary of the findings is presented here.

The most consistent finding of the small group process-product research is that giving explanations is positively correlated with achievement, partialling out ability (Swing and Peterson, 1982; Webb, 1980; Webb, in press a, in press c; Webb and Kenderski, 1982). This conforms to the frequently reported finding that peer tutors learn by teaching others (see, for example, Devin-Sheehan, Feldman, and Allen, 1976). On the other hand, *receiving* help has been more infrequently found to relate to achievement (Webb, 1980; Webb, in press c). Receiving help is associated with greater achievement, controlling for ability, primarily when the help received was an explanation. There was a strong negative relationship between achievement and receiving no response to a question or receiving an answer without an explanation (Webb, in press a, in press c; Webb and Kenderski, 1982). If there is a single principle to be gleaned from the process-product research on small group learning, it is that explanations, either given or received, lead to increased achievement.

Chapter Summary: Cooperative Learning and Student Achievement

The research summarized in this chapter includes all methodologically adequate studies of cooperative learning methods in elementary or secondary classrooms implemented over periods of at least two weeks known to the author. The results of this research justifies the following conclusions:

1. Looking at the field experimental studies as a whole, the effects of cooperative learning on student achievement have been quite positive. Of forty-one studies conducted in regular classrooms, 26 (63%) have found significantly positive achievement effects

favoring the cooperative learning groups, and only one found greater learning in a control group.

2. Among the cooperative learning methods in which all students study the same material, methods that provide *specific group rewards based on members' learning* are much more likely to be associated with greater achievement gain than control groups than those that do not. Of 25 studies in which groups were rewarded based on their members' learning, 22 (88%) found positive effects on student achievement, while none of nine studies that did not use such group rewards found positive achievement results. Three component analyses (Huber, Bogatzki, and Winter, 1982; Hulten and DeVries, 1976; Slavin, 1980a) also found that group rewards, but not group tasks, are critical to the achievement effects of cooperative learning.

3. Use of *task specialization* (where group members are responsible for unique portions of the group task) may be an effective procedure for increasing student achievement, at least in certain areas of social studies, but the evidence concerning this is unclear at present.

4. Cooperative learning methods high in *individual accountability* of group members to their groupmates are much more likely to produce greater learning than control methods that are cooperative learning methods low in individual accountability. No study in which group members worked together to produce a single worksheet or group product has found positive achievement effects.

5. There is no evidence that use of *group competition* affects student achievement differently from any other means of providing specific group rewards based on members' learning.

6. Use of *equal opportunity scoring* systems may enhance the achievement effects of cooperative learning, but the evidence is not yet conclusive.

7. While *ability by treatment interactions* are inconsistent in size and direction, *race by treatment interactions* tend to indicate that blacks (and possibly Hispanics) gain more from cooperative learning than Anglos.

8. Process-product studies indicate that *giving and receiving explanations* (as opposed to providing answers or making no response to questions) are positively related to learning in small groups. Receiving no answers or answers without explanation are negatively related to achievement.

Based on the evidence of the field experiments reviewed in this chapter, it can be concluded that the effects of cooperative learning on achievement are primarily *motivational* effects, not *process* effects; cooperative incentive structures, not task structures, explain the effects of cooperative learning on achievement. That is, little evidence supports any positive effect on the achievement of students in general of working in small groups. However, a great deal of evidence supports the contention that working with others to achieve a group goal, where the criterion for group success is the sum of the group members' learning performance, does increase student achievement. The dependence of students on one anothers' learning apparently creates peer norms supporting learning, and these in turn increase the individuals' motivations to achieve and to help one another achieve. The available evidence points to this chain of causality as the principle means by which cooperative learning increases student achievement.

4

Cooperative Learning and Intergroup Relations

For the past thirty years, school desegregation has been one of the most important and controversial social issues on the American scene. From early on, psychologists, sociologists, and other social scientists have studied school desegregation and desegregation in the larger society to understand their effects. At present, social science has reached a somewhat pessimistic consensus about the effects of school desegregation on student achievement and race relations, although few have argued that desegregation has negative effects on these outcomes. A review by Crain and Mahard (1978) concluded that the achievement of black students is increased somewhat by desegregation, but the effects are small and are seen only under certain conditions. On the other hand, such reviewers as St. John (1975), Stephen (1978), and Cohen (1975) have concluded that neither achievement nor race relations are improved by desegregation.

In the case of race relations, the failure to find positive effects seems on first thought to be puzzling. How can it be that students of different races who have a chance to interact do not form friendships over time and come to accept each other? Yet the evidence against markedly improved relationships across race lines is strong. In a recent analyses of data from the National Assessment of Educational Progress, involving more than 18,000 students, Scott and McPartland (in press) found tiny positive effects of desegregation on racial attitudes at the third grade level, and no effects at all at junior or senior high school levels. Gerard and Miller (1975) found in another large study that friendships across ethnic-group lines actually decreased over the years students attended desegregated schools. Many smaller studies have similarly tended to find small positive, small negative, or more often no effects of school desegregation on race relations.

But desegregation must be seen as an opportunity, not a cure. Cook (1979), who participated in the deliberations that led to the famous Social Science Statement (Minnesota Law Review, 1953) that played a part in the 1954 *Brown vs. Board of Education* decision, has pointed out that social scientists thirty years ago knew that school desegregation must be accompanied by changes in school practices if there were to be positive effects of desegregation on relationships between black and white students.

The Social Science Statement was an appendix to appellants' briefs filed in the Supreme Court's school desegregation cases, including *Brown*, in 1952. The Statement reviewed the social science evidence then available to anticipate the effects of desegregation on black students. It was signed by thirty-two social scientists who were then or were to become the leaders of American social science. In 1952, these social scientists had had little experience with school desegregation, but they were able to draw on examples of desegregation in the armed forces, housing, and employment. The experience of desegregation and race relations led the social scientists to be cautiously optimistic about predicting positive effects of desegregation on race relations among students, but they knew that the *conditions* under which interracial contact takes place are critical to the outcome. They wrote:

> Under certain circumstances desegregation not only proceeds without major difficulties, but has been observed to lead to the emergence of more favorable attitudes and friendlier relations between races. . . . Much depends, however, on the circumstances under which members of previously segregated groups first came in contact with others in unsegregated situations.
>
> Available evidence suggests . . . the importance of consistent and firm enforcement of the new policy by those in authority. It indicates also the importance of such factors as: the absence of competition for a limited number of facilities or benefits; the possibility of contacts which permit individuals to learn about one another as individuals; and the possibility of equivalence of positions and functions among all of the participants within the unsegregated situation. (*Minnesota Law Review*, 1953, pp. 437–438)

This section was based on the work of Gordon Allport, one of the signers of the Social Science Statement. Allport himself, in *The Nature of Prejudice* (1954), made more explicit the importance of the context of interracial contact. He cited research that indicated that superficial contact could damage race relations, as could competitive contact and contact between individuals of markedly different status. However, he also cited evidence to the effect that when individuals of different racial or ethnic groups worked to achieve common goals, when they had opportunities to get to know one another as individuals, and when they worked with one another on an equal footing, they became friends and did not continue to hold prejudices against one another. Allport's contact theory of intergroup relations, based on these findings, has dominated social science inquiry in race relations for three decades. His own summary of the essentials of contact theory is as follows:

> Prejudice . . . may be reduced by equal status contact between majority and minority groups in the pursuit of common goals. The effect is greatly enhanced

if this contact is sanctioned by institutional supports . . . and if it is of a sort that leads to the perception of common interests and common humanity between members of the two groups. (Allport, 1954, p. 281)

Traditional school organization hardly fulfills the conditions outlined by Allport and by the Social Science Statement. Interaction between students of different ethnicities is typically competitive and superficial. Black, Anglo, Hispanic, and other groups compete for grades, for teacher approval, for places on the student council and the cheerleading squad. Students have little chance for indepth contact. In the classroom, the one setting in which students of different races or ethnicities are likely to be at least sitting side by side, traditional instructional methods permit little contact between students that is not superficial. Otherwise, since black, Anglo, and Hispanic students usually ride different busses to different neighborhoods, participate in different kinds of activities, and go to different social functions, opportunities for positive intergroup interaction are limited. One major exception is sports; sports teams in integrated schools are almost always integrated. Sports teams create conditions of cooperation and non-superficial contact among team members, and correlational research by Slavin and Madden (1979) has shown that students who participated in sports in desegregated high schools were much more likely to have friends outside of their own race group and to have positive racial attitudes than were students who did not participate in integrated sports teams. In fact, the Slavin and Madden (1979) study of fifty-one high schools found no consistent effects of such traditional race relations programs as teaching of minority history, workshops for teachers, or use of textbooks showing minority individuals in positive roles. The only consistent findings were that students who reported having participated in integrated sports teams or classroom work groups were much more likely than those who did not to have positive racial attitudes and to report having friends outside of their own race groups.

The cooperative learning methods described in Chapter 2 are one solution to the problem of providing students of different races and ethnicities with opportunities to have non-superficial, cooperative interaction. Cooperative learning methods specifically use the strength of the desegregated school, the presence of students of different races or ethnicities, to enhance intergroup relations. As noted in Chapter 2, the groups in which students work in these methods are made up of four to five students of different races, sexes, and levels of achievement, with each group reflecting the composition of the class as a whole in these attributes. The groups usually receive rewards, recognition, and/or evaluation based on the degree to which they can increase the academic performance of each of the members of the group. This is in sharp contrast to the interstudent competition for grades and teacher approval characteristic of the traditional classroom. Cooperation between students is emphasized by the classroom rewards and tasks and by the teacher, who tries to communicate an "all for one, one for all" attitude. The structures of most of the cooperative learning methods also attempt to insure each student a chance to make a substantial contribution to the team, so that teammates will be equal, at least in the sense of role equality specified by Allport (1954). The cooperative learning methods are designed to be true changes in classroom organization, not time limited "treatments." They provide daily opportunities for intense interpersonal contact between students of different races. When the teacher assigns students of different races or ethnicities to work together, this communicates unequivocal support on the part of the teacher for the idea that interracial or interethnic interaction is officially sanctioned. Even though race or race relations per se need never be mentioned (and rarely are) in the course of cooperative learning experiences, it is difficult for a student to believe that his or her teacher believes in racial separation when the teacher has assigned the class to multiethnic teams.

Thus, at least in theory, cooperative learning methods satisfy the conditions outlined in the Social Science Statement and by Allport (1954) for positive effects of desegregation on race relations: interracial cooperation; equal status roles for students of different races; contact across race lines that permits students to learn about one another as individuals; and the communication of unequivocal teacher support for interracial contact.

Research on Cooperative Learning and Intergroup Relations.

The methods evaluated for effects on intergroup relations are a subset of those studied for achievement effects (see Chapter 3), with the addition of a study by Weigel, Wiser, and Cook (1975). The same criteria used for the achievement studies to discriminate field experiments from laboratory studies in field settings were used for the intergroup relations studies. Experiments of two week's duration or more, conducted in elementary or secondary classrooms, and using appropriate research methods and analyses to rule out obvious bias are highlighted in this chapter. Most of the studies used sociometric (e.g., "Who are your friends in this class?"), peer rating, or behavioral observation measures to measure intergroup relations as pairwise positive relations between individuals of different ethnic backgrounds. A few studies operationalized intergroup relations as attitudes toward various ethnic groups. Several studies used such sociometric questions as "Who have you helped in this class?" Because only students in the cooperative learning classes are likely to have helped their classmates, this and related measures are biased toward the cooperative learning treatments, so the results of these measures are not presented in this chapter. Also, observations of cross-racial interaction during the treatment classes—another measure of implementation rather than outcome—are not presented.

TABLE 4.1 Characteristics and Intergroup Relations Outcomes of Cooperative Learning Field Experiments

Major Reports	No. of Students	Grade Level	Duration (weeks)	Level of Random Assignment	Kind of School	Ethnic Composition	Type of Measure	Intergroup Relations Effects
Group Study, Group Reward for Learning Methods								
Student Teams-Achievement Divisions (STAD)								
Slavin, 1977c	62	7	10	class	Urban East	B-61% W-39%	Sociometric	+
Slavin, 1979; Hansell and Slavin, 1981	424	7–8	12	class	Urban East	W-61% B-39%	Sociometric	+
Slavin and Oickle, 1981	230	6–8	12	class	Rural East	W-66% B-34%	Sociometric	Black-White Friendships 0 White-Black Friendships +
Teams-Games-Tournament (TGT) DeVries, Edwards and Slavin, 1979:								
Experiment 1	96	7	9	class	Urban East	W-70% B-30%	Sociometric	0
Experiment 2	128	7	12	student	Urban East	B-51% W-49%	Sociometric	+
Experiment 3	191	10–12	12	class	Suburban South	W-90% B-10%	Sociometric	+
Experiment 4 (also reported as as DeVries and Edwards, 1974)	117	7	4	student	Urban East	W-57% B-43%	Sociometric	+

Group Study Methods

	N	Grade	Duration	Unit	Composition	Location	Measure	Outcome
Learning Together								
Cooper, Johnson, Johnson, and Wilderson, 1980	57	7	3	student	W-67% B-33%	Urban Midwest	Sociometric	+
Johnson and Johnson, 1981	51	4	3	student	W-78% B-18% H-2% AI-2%	Urban Midwest	Observation	+
Weigel, Wiser, and Cook Methods								
Weigel, Wiser, and Cook, 1975	324	7–10	Gr.7- 28 wks. Gr. 10- 18 wks.	class	W-71% B-17% H-12%	Urban West	Peer rating	Ratings of: -Hispanics + -Blacks 0 -Whites 0
							Sociometric	Friendships toward: -Hispanics + -Blacks 0 -Whites 0
							Ethnic Attitudes	0

Task Specialization, Group Reward for Learning Methods

	N	Grade	Duration	Unit	Composition	Location	Measure	Outcome
Jigsaw II								
Ziegler, 1981	146	6	8	class	AC-44% E-36% A-12% WI-8%	Urban Canada	Sociometric Ethnic Attitudes	+ +

TABLE 4.1 *(continued)*

Major Reports	No. of Students	Grade Level	Duration (weeks)	Level of Random Assignment	Kind of School	Ethnic Composition	Type of Measure	Intergroup Relations Effects
					Task Specialization Methods			
Jigsaw								
Blaney, Stephan, Rosenfield, Aronson, and Sikes, 1977	304	5–6	6	Non-Random (matched)	Urban Southwest	W-59% B-23% H-16% A-2%	Sociometric	0
Gonzales, 1979	326	9–12	10	Non-Random (matched)	Calif. Rural Town	W-48% H-44% A-6% B-1%	Ethnic Attitudes	Ratings of: −Hispanics + −Asians 0 −Anglos 0
Gonzales, 1981	182	3–4	20	Non-Random (matched)	Rural Calif. (bilingual classes)	H-54% W-46%	Ethnic Attitudes	0

+ Cooperative learning group exceeded control group significantly ($p < .05$)
0 No significant differences

W = Non-Hispanic whites   A = Asian-Americans   WI = West Indian Immigrants
B = Blacks   AC = Anglo-Canadians   AI = American Indians
H = Hispanic-Americans   E = European Immigrants

Note: Please see text for explanations of findings.

Table 4.1 summarizes the characteristics and outcomes of the cooperative learning studies. Note that all of the Student Team Learning studies (STAD, TGT, Jigsaw II) plus the Gonzales (1981) Jigsaw study also appeared in Table 3.2 as achievement studies, although the intergroup relations results were often presented in different articles.

In Table 4.1, a "+" in the right-hand column indicates a statistically significant ($p<.05$) difference between the cooperative learning group and the control group on the indicated measure. In some cases, positive effects were found for attitudes of friendships toward one ethnic group, but not toward others. When no differences were found, a "0" appears in the table. For intergroup relations outcomes, no effects favoring control groups have been found.

Main Effects on Intergroup Relations

The experimental evidence on cooperative learning has generally supported the conclusions of the Social Science Statement and of Allport (1954). With only a few exceptions, this research has demonstrated that when the conditions outlined by Allport are met in the classroom, students are more likely to have friends outside of their own race groups than they are in traditional classrooms, as measured by responses to such sociometric items as "Who are your best friends in this class?"

The evidence linking STAD to gains in cross-racial friendships is strong. In two studies, Slavin (1977c, 1979) found that students who had experienced STAD over periods of 10–12 weeks gained more in cross-racial friendships than did control students. Slavin and Oickle (1981) found significant gains in white friendships toward blacks as a consequence of STAD, but found no differences in black friendships toward whites. The Slavin (1979) study included a followup into the next academic year, in which students who had been in the experimental and control classes were asked to list their friends. Students who had been in the control group listed an average of less than one friend of another race, or 9.8% of all of their friendship choices; those who had been in the experimental group named an average of 2.4 friends outside of their own race groups, 37.9% of their friendship choices. The STAD research covered grades 6–8, and took place in schools ranging from 34% to 61% black.

DeVries, Edwards, and Slavin (1978) summarized data analyses from four studies of TGT in desegregated schools. In three of these, students who had been in classes that used TGT gained significantly more in friends outside of their own race groups than did control students. In one, no differences were found. The samples involved in these studies varied in grade levels from 7–12 and in percent minority students from 10% to 51%.

The effects of the original Jigsaw method on intergroup relations are more uncertain than those for STAD and TGT. Blaney, Stephan, Rosenfield, Aronson, and Sikes (1977) did find that students in desegregated classes using Jigsaw preferred their groupmates to their other classmates in general. However, as students' groupmates and their other classmates were about the same in ethnic composition, this cannot be seen as a measure of intergroup relations. No differences between the experimental and control groups in interethnic friendship choices were found (Rosenfield, personal communication). Gonzales (1979), using a method similar to Jigsaw, found that Anglo and Asian-American students had better attitudes towards Mexican-American classmates in the Jigsaw groups than in control groups, but he found no differences in attitudes toward Anglo or Asian-American students. In a subsequent study, Gonzales (1981) found no differences in attitudes toward Mexican-Americans, blacks, or Anglos between Jigsaw and control bilingual classes. The most positive effects of a Jigsaw-related intervention were found in a study of Jigsaw II by Ziegler (1981) in classes composed of recent European and West Indian immigrants and Anglo-Canadians in Toronto. She found substantially more cross-ethnic friendships in the Jigsaw II classes than in control classes both on an immediate posttest and on a ten-week followup. These effects were both for "casual friendships" ("Who in this class would you call your friends?") and for "close friendships" ("Who in this class have you called on the telephone in the last two weeks?" and "Who in this class have you spent time with after school in the last two weeks?")

Two Learning Together studies have examined intergroup relations outcomes. Cooper, Johnson, Johnson, and Wilderson (1980) found greater friendship across race lines in a cooperative treatment than in an individualized method in which students were not permitted to interact. However, there were no differences in cross-racial friendships between the cooperative condition and a competitive condition in which students competed with equals (similar to the TGT tournaments). Johnson and Johnson (1981) found more cross-racial interaction in cooperative than in individualized classes during free time. The Johnson and Johnson (1981) study is important because, unlike nearly all of the studies of cooperative learning and intergroup relations, which depend entirely on self-reported sociometric data, they actually observed black-white interaction in school. Students were observed during ten-minute free time periods immediately following either a cooperative intervention or an individualistic intervention (in which students were forbidden to interact). Black and white students in cooperative classes interacted far more frequently than students in the individualistic classes during their free time activities. However, it is unclear whether these results have meaning outside of the classroom setting, as students in the cooperative condition may have simply stayed in their integrated groups during the observation sessions, and as students in traditionally taught classes are typically allowed to interact more than were students in the Johnson and Johnson (1981) and Cooper et al. (1980) individualistic control groups.

One of the largest and longest studies of cooperative learning was conducted by Weigel, Wiser, and Cook (1975) in tri-ethnic (Mexican-American, Anglo, black) classrooms. They evaluated a method in which students in multi-ethnic teams engaged in a variety of cooperative activities in several subjects, winning prizes based on their team performance. They reported that their cooperative methods had positive effects on white attitudes toward Mexican-Americans, but not on white-black, black-white, black-Hispanic, Hispanic-black, or Hispanic-white attitudes. They also found that cooperative learning reduced teachers' reports of interethnic conflict.

The effects of cooperative learning methods reviewed here are not entirely consistent, but eleven of the fourteen studies demonstrated that when the conditions of contact theory are fulfilled, some aspect of friendship between students of different ethnicities improves.

The pattern of findings in studies in which not all of the hypothesized effects were found is an interesting one. In three cases (Blaney et al., 1977; DeVries, Edwards, and Slavin, 1978; Gonzales, 1981), no intergroup relations effects were found. However, in three other studies (Slavin and Oickle, 1981; Weigel, Wiser, and Cook, 1975; Gonzales, 1979), positive effects of cooperative learning were found for attitudes toward or friendships with one of the ethnic groups but not the other(s). In each of these studies, positive effects were found for majority attitudes toward minority students, but not for minority-majority attitudes. This may indicate that minority group members usually begin with better attitudes toward majority group individuals than the other way around (cf. Slavin and Madden, 1979), but this trend needs to be explored in greater depth before firm conclusions can be drawn (see Slavin and Oickle, 1981).

It is important to note that in all but one of the studies of cooperative learning in which both achievement and intergroup relations were measured, achievement increased more in the cooperative groups than the control groups. All four of the TGT studies (Edwards, DeVries, and Snyder, 1972; Edwards and DeVries, 1972, 1974; DeVries, Edwards, and Wells, 1974) found positive effects on achievement as well as race relations, as did two of the three STAD studies (Slavin, 1977c; Slavin and Oickle, 1981). The Ziegler (1981) study of Jigsaw II found positive achievement effects, as well as the previously noted effects on cross-ethnic friendships.

Thus it is apparent that cooperative learning does positively affect relationships between students of different races or ethnicities, while also increasing their achievement. In terms of implications for educational practice, these main effects are the most important findings of the research on cooperative learning. However, it may be possible to further improve these techniques, and better understand how intergroup relations are formed in schools, if we can discover how and why cooperative learning methods improve intergroup relations.

Contact Theory in the Classroom

As noted above, the theory linking cooperative learning methods to improvements in intergroup relations is derived from Allport's (1954) contact theory. Contact theory has been studied in the social psychological laboratory for many years (see, for example, Cook, 1978). The field experimental research on cooperative learning methods in the classroom offers a new opportunity to explore many of the components and assumptions behind contact theory. Clearly, the cooperative learning research confirms the expectation that a treatment based on contact theory would improve intergroup relations. The following sections consider how cooperative learning affects the conditions for contact, cooperation, equal status, and normative climate in the classroom, which are major dimensions of contact theory.

How Close are the New Cross-Ethnic Friendships?   It is not surprising that friendships across racial or ethnic boundaries are rare relative to friendships within these groups. Black, Hispanic, and Anglo students typically live in different neighborhoods, ride different busses, and prefer different activities. Secondary students of different ethnicities often come from different elementary schools. Socioeconomic, sex, and achievement differences further separate students. These factors work against friendship formation even when race is not a factor (see Lott and Lott, 1965). Racial differences accentuate the tendencies for students to form homogeneous peer groups, and sometimes result in overt prejudice and interracial hostility.

Given the many forces operating against the formation of cross-racial friendships, it would seem that if cooperative learning influences these friendships, it would affect relatively weak relationships rather than strong relationships. Strong relationships take more time, involve more emotional intensity and intimacy, and are based on more reciprocal communications and exchanges of rewards than weak relationships (Granovetter, 1973). On first thought, it seems unlikely that a few weeks of cooperative learning would increase strong interracial relationships between students in the classroom at the possible expense of pre-existing same-race relationships.

A study by Hansell and Slavin (1981) investigated this hypothesis. Their sample included seventh- and eighth-grade students in 12 inner-city language arts classrooms. Classes were randomly assigned to cooperative learning (STAD) or control treatments for a ten-week program. Students were asked on both pre- and posttests, "Who are your best friends in this class? Name as many as you wish," in a free-choice format. The study used two measures of the strength of student friendships—reciprocity and choice order. Hallinan (1979) has suggested that students typically name about six or seven best friends on sociometric questionnaires. Choices were defined as "close" if they were among the first six made by students, and "distant" if they occurred seventh or later. Close choices tend to be more

TABLE 4.2   Standardized Betas for STAD Effects on Cross-Race Choices Made and Received

| | | Type of Cross-Race Choice: | | |
	Close	Distant	Reciprocated	Unreciprocated
Made (N = 204)	.17*	.11	.25*	.06
Received (N = 267)	.15*	.15*	.25*	.04

* Beta is statistically significant, *p*<.05

NOTE: Standardized betas were obtained in equations controlling for student achievement, sex, race, and number of pretest choices, and classroom racial composition. Positive signs of all betas indicate STAD classes were higher than control classes (see text). Adapted from Hansell and Slavin (1981, p. 103).

stable than distant choices (Hallinan, 1979; Moreno, 1934) and tend to be reciprocated. The reciprocity and order of choices made and received were analyzed with multiple regressions, controlling for total pretest choices made or received, achievement, sex, race, and classroom racial composition. The results of these analyses are presented in Table 4.2.

The results show that the positive effects of STAD on cross-racial choices were primarily due to increases in strong friendship choices. Reciprocated and close choices, both made and received, increased as a result of the treatment. In addition, there was a significant increase in distant choices received, but there were no significant changes in other types of weak friendship relations. Thus, contrary to what might have been expected, this study showed positive cooperative learning effects on close, reciprocated friendship choices, the kind of friendships that should be most difficult to change.

Cooperation vs. Contact Per Se.   Allport's (1954) research documented many cases in which contract between the races did not improve racial attitudes. School desegregation brings students of different ethnicities into regular interpersonal contact of some kind, but does not lead by itself to improvements in intergroup relations (Gerard and Miller, 1975; St. John, 1975; Stephan, 1978). Thus it is clear that not all interracial contact leads to favorable relations.

Allport (1954) emphasized that if interracial contract is to improve race relations, the contact should be cooperative rather than competitive. Later research (e.g., Johnson and Johnson, 1972) has shown that individuals working toward a cooperative goal come to like each other, at least in part because individuals like others who help them achieve important goals. In a cooperative group, each group member's efforts help the group to be rewarded, so the group members themselves are seen in a positive light by their groupmates.

However, it is difficult to separate the effects of cooperation from the effects of contact per se. When cooperative learning is introduced in a desegregated classroom, interracial interaction is drastically increased (Johnson and Johnson, 1981; Slavin and Wodarski, 1978). As students interact every day for many weeks, it is only logical to expect that many of them will become friends. But is it the interaction that produces the cross-racial friendships, or does the cooperative goal make an independent contribution to friendship formation?

There is some evidence that the critical variable is contact, not cooperation. Cook (1978) found that when poor, southern nursery school mothers who had had very few interracial contacts in the past participated in weekly mixed discussion groups, cross-racial friendships tended to increase regardless of whether or not the groups were structured cooperatively.

Cooper, Johnson, Johnson, and Wilderson (1980) compared the Learning Together model to competitive and individualistic methods. In the competitive condition, students were assigned to equal-ability clusters, and received praise for being the best in their cluster. In the individualistic condition, students were forbidden to interact, and received individual praise. In this study, a much higher percentage of students in the cooperative and competitive conditions made friendship choices outside of their own racial groups than did students in the individualistic condition. However, there were no differences between the cooperative and competitive conditions; in fact, the proportion of students making cross-racial choices was somewhat higher in the competitive group than in the cooperative group.

This result would support a conclusion that it is assigning students to groups in which they may interact, not cooperative goals, that produces the effect on intergroup reactions. This result directly contradicts Allport's emphasis on cooperation (or at least non-competition) as a criterion for positive outcomes of interracial contact. However, there are other issues involved. The cooperative groups in the Cooper et al. study were heterogeneous on academic ability, while the competitive "clusters" were homogeneous. Assuming that the "clusters" were racially mixed (this is not stated), the homogeneous assignment might have created interaction between the black and white students most likely to become friends, those of similar academic achievement. The positive effects of this homogeneous cluster assignment on the chances of friendships forming across race lines may have offset any negative effect of the competition. Also, competition in Allport's sense refers to a serious struggle for limited resources. Both the cooperation and the competition applied by Cooper et al. (1980) were mild and diffuse; had substantial rewards or grades been attached to success in both conditions, the results might have been quite different. In fact, a series of laboratory studies by Cook (1978) and his associates implied that if success in a cooperative group was available to all groups, use of substantial group rewards led to greater attraction among group members than did group cooperation without reward, the situation in the Cooper et al. study. From the students' points of view, the primary difference between the cooperative and competitive treatments might have been the homogeneous vs. heterogeneous group assignment, not the difference in how rewards were assigned.

At present, the relative importance of contact per se vs. cooperative contact for intergroup relations in schools is unclear. On one hand, it seems likely that if regular, positive, equal-status interracial interaction can be created in a school setting, relationships between individuals of different races will be good. Holding that level of interaction constant, cooperative group goals may or may not add to the effect. However, cooperative goals increase the level and quality of interpersonal interaction (see Johnson and Johnson, 1974); in other words, if high-quality non-superficial contact can be created by any means, race relations are likely to be improved, but setting cooperative tasks and goals may well be the most efficient way to bring about this level of positive interaction.

In the classroom, this last point may be particularly critical. It is difficult to imagine a classroom intervention that would be usable over the long term and that would be likely to create frequent, positive interracial interaction, but would not involve some form of cooperation. Further, there is evidence that well-structured cooperative tasks and clearly specified cooperative rewards are needed to create maximal peer interaction. Slavin (1980a) compared STAD to a condition in which students could study with anyone in the class, but no rewards were given for doing well as a group. Despite the fact that the students in this condition were more likely to be with friends than were the students in the teacher-assigned heterogeneous STAD groups, peer interaction was substantially higher in the STAD condition.

The different results obtained for the Jigsaw and Jigsaw II studies may also argue for the importance of group goals. In the three Jigsaw studies (Blaney et al., 1977; Gonzales, 1979, 1981), no group rewards were given. Students were interdependent because they depended on each other's information to do well on tests, but they were individually graded. Only one of these studies (Gonzales, 1979) found even partial positive effects on intergroup relations. In contrast, Ziegler (1981) gave students grades based in part on their group performance, and found positive intergroup relations effects that were both strong and long lasting.

Thus, a laissez-faire form of peer interaction may not be enough to produce high levels of positive interpersonal interaction in the classroom. A structured group intervention with clear group goals and rewards may be the most practical means of creating frequent non-superficial interracial contact in the classroom, so despite the theoretical importance of contact per se vs. cooperative tasks and goals, this distinction may have little meaning in practice.

Group Competition vs. Group Non-Competition

One issue that has provoked a lively and continuing debate among cooperative learning researchers is the issue of group competition vs. pure cooperation. Slavin (1981a), for example, defends the use of competition between learning groups as a practical means of motivating students to cooperate within learning groups. However, Johnson (1981) criticizes such mixed strategies as unnecessary and potentially harmful, and Weigel, Wiser, and Cook (1975), who used group competition in their study, questioned whether group competition might inflame status-based rivalries.

The examples Allport (1954) cites to support his emphasis on cooperative contact as a precondition of positive race relations (e.g., sports teams, military platoons in battle) involve intergroup competition, not pure cooperation. However, in theory as well as in the actual research, it is clear that group competition is not necessary; any superordinate goal should produce similar effects. In Sherif and Sherif's (1953) classic Robber's Cave experiment, intense group rivalry was not broken down when the groups attended a party together, but was dissipated when the groups had to cooperate to perform a task that benefitted both groups, pulling their bus out of the mud. In later research, Sherif (1961) used small group competition to achieve the same results. What is apparently critical in each case is not group competition, but whether or not there is a salient, important group goal with some kind of group reward (or an external threat). There is evidence that cohesiveness increases as group rewards increase. Cook (1978) found that providing groups with a monetary reward increased their acceptance of a black group member (an experimental confederate) when the group was told that it was successful. When the group was told that it was unsuccessful in earning the reward, the acceptance of the black member was no lower than in cases when no group reward was given. Presumably, if groups were occasionally rewarded (as in a fair group competition), their cohesiveness and interracial acceptance would be higher than if no rewards were given. Studies of group competition bear this out. For example, Myers (1962) found that when recreational rifle teams were in competition with other teams, their cohesiveness was higher than when they were simply trying to exceed a standard. Rabbie and Horwitz (1969) found that losers as well as winners in group competition gained more in liking for their groupmates than did similar groups not faced with a win-lose situation.

However, it is probably not group competition per se that explains these results, but provision of group rewards, where group competition is simply the basis on which rewards are given to groups. In this case, it is probably not specific group rewards based on members' learning that are needed, but simply a group reward that can only be achieved when students work together or perform separate roles adequately. Under these circumstances, each individual's efforts potentially bring rewards to all group members, and positive relationships are likely to form when individuals are rewarding to one another (see Lott and Lott, 1965). Group competition may be the most practical means of providing meaningful group rewards, as recognition is the easiest group reward to use. Many alternative forms of group reward have practical drawbacks. For example, grades based on group scores, a method advocated by Deutsch (1979) and by Johnson and Johnson (1975), has serious ethical problems over the long run, because high achievers in low-achieving groups can legitimately complain of unfair grading. Payments to groups would be even less acceptable to most schools. Recognition only makes sense if there is a meaningful standard, and group competition is an obvious way to provide such a standard. It is possible to reward groups for exceeding a preset criterion, as was done by Madden and Slavin (in press) and by Slavin, Leavey, and Madden (1982), but if the scores themselves are made public, students and teachers tend to interpret this situation as group competition. There is no evidence that group competition is deleterious to intergroup relations, but it would still be interesting to evaluate cooperative methods that involve adequate group rewards without group competition.

Equal Status. One of Allport's (1954) theoretical criteria for contact to improve intergroup relations is that it occurs between individuals of equal status. Equal status has been emphasized by many in recent years as a critical aspect of contact theory as it relates to school desegregation (see, for example, Amir, 1969; Cohen, 1975). In Allport's use of the term, students in the same grade level have "equal status," regardless of race, sex, or achievement level. Allport was concerned more with occupational and socio-economic status than with status associated with ascribed characteristics or innate abilities. The kind of equal status studied by Allport (1954) is referred to by Cook (1960) as "situational equal status."

However, Cohen's (1975) research introduces a new meaning to the term equal status. She is interested in the perceptions of competence which students of different ethnicities have about each other, and whether students of different races and ethnicities have equal performance expectations for each other. In Cohen's sense, equal status may be impossible to achieve in an American school, because blacks are often seen as lower in competence, and low expectations for blacks by whites generalize beyond situations in which they may in fact be lower in achievement. Cohen states:

> The inference may be drawn that even though blacks and whites might be brought together in a desegregated school in an "equal status" manner, it is still quite possible for the racial difference to act as a strong status differential triggering expectations for whites to do better in a new situation and for blacks to do less well. If this occurs in the school situation, then the racial stereotypes which contribute to these expectations are only reinforced and confirmed by the interracial interaction in the desegregated school. It should be a matter of great concern if the process of desegregation actually does result in reinforcing such stereotype of racial incompetence. (1975, p. 294).

The implication of Cohen's argument is that equal-status interaction between black and white students is unlikely, particularly when actual black-white differences in reading and mathematics performance confirm racial stereotypes. On many occasions, Cohen has voiced a concern that placing students in small work groups would make racial achievement differences even more salient, thereby diminishing any chance that black and white students might treat one another as equals.

If, as Cohen suggests, minority students are perceived as less competent, then they should be less well liked by their groupmates as a consequence of a cooperative learning intervention. However, the data from the field experiments on cooperative learning directly contradicts this expectation. As noted earlier, improvements in majority-minority friendships are even more consistently seen than are increases in minority-majority friendships.

There are several possible reasons that Cohen's predictions are not borne out by the data. First, her demonstrations that whites have low performance expectations for blacks (e.g., Cohen and Roper, 1972) involve one-time observations in laboratory settings. Having had the experience of working together in small groups over a longer period of time, white students might learn that their black groupmates do in fact have much to contribute to the group, and are no less able than themselves. Even though black students often score less well than whites on many tests, tracking in class assignments often places together black and white students who are similar in achievement level. Even when there are differences in the average achievement levels of blacks and whites in the same class, there will be blacks among the highest-performing students and whites among the lowest-performing students, making a racial generalization difficult to make. Further, two studies of STAD (Slavin, 1977b; Slavin and Oickle, 1981) found that initial significant achievement differences between black and white students were eliminated in the STAD groups while they remained in the control groups, suggesting that even if there are perceptible racial differences in achievement, the experience of working in cooperative groups may erase them.

Another reason that Cohen's fears about cooperative learning have not been realized may be that the most frequently evaluated cooperative learning methods, STAD, TGT, and Jigsaw II, use equal opportunity scoring systems intended to diminish the salience or effect of ability differences within the cooperative activities. For example, the use of improvement scores in STAD makes sure that no student is automatically a drag on the team score.

At present, the evidence about the role of equal status and of equal-opportunity scoring in cooperative learning interventions is unclear. Unfortunately, cooperative learning researchers have not measured status perceptions directly, and Cohen and her colleagues have not measured race relations. It seems unlikely that positive race relations absolutely require equal performance status (as opposed to situational status) between blacks and whites, but future research could establish this link.

Institution Norms. Allport (1954) hypothesized that cross-racial contact would be more likely to improve race relations if the institutions in which the contact took place clearly supported racial interaction and racial equality. Allport felt that most whites had conflicting feelings about desegregation. On the one hand they may be uncomfortable about interacting with blacks or others different from themselves, but on the other hand they feel shame about this discomfort, because most Americans believe in fair play and equality. Allport therefore reasoned that whites accepted desegregation best when they themselves did not have to initiate interracial contact, and when such contact was forcefully mandated by institutional norms and policies.

In schools, one might assume that institutional support for interracial contact would always be present. Certainly, few school officials openly advocate segregation. However, teachers and administrators are often quite uncomfortable about the issue of race, being unsure whether race should simply be ignored ("We're all the same here") or whether race relations should be openly discussed and dealt with. Students may get the idea that while racial conflicts are not permitted in school, positive cross-racial contacts are not really encouraged either.

One simple change that cooperative learning methods may make in the desegregated classroom is to clearly legitimate positive interracial contact. Students of different races may hold few overt prejudices, but still be reluctant to take the first step toward making friends of another race. Such students might welcome having the teacher establish a normative climate that supports and encourages interracial interaction, and labels it as normal and desirable. This climate may be created without a word about race being spoken; the fact that the teacher assigns students to racially mixed learning groups clearly indicates teacher approval of interracial interaction. Had the teacher allowed students to choose their own teams (which would often result in racially and sexually homogeneous teams), the opposite message might be communicated.

There is no research at present that bears directly on the issue of institutional support as a possible contributor to the effects of cooperative learning on intergroup relations, and this effect might be difficult to separate from the effects of contact per se. However, this may be an important issue for a theory of cooperative learning and intergroup relations.

Perceived Similarity. One of the strongest determinants of friendship in general (after contact) is a perception on the part of two individuals that they share important characteristics, world views, favorite activities, and so on (see Lott and Lott, 1965). One problem of race relations is that students of different races or ethnicities are likely to be dissimilar on many important attributes, such as socioeconomic status, values, and preferred activities; even if students could be made color-blind, these differences would be likely to continue the tendency for students to make friends primarily within their own race groups.

Allport (1954) referred to perceived similarity as a criterion for contact to lead to improved race relations in his emphasis on equal status and on cross-racial contact that "leads to a perception of common interests and common humanity." However, few of the basic racial dissimilarities which are likely to exist in desegregated classrooms can be easily overcome.

In one sense, cooperative learning methods create a new basis of perceived similarity among relatively dissimilar students. The act of assigning students to teams automatically gives them a common identity. Social psychological laboratory research has shown that simply announcing group assignments induced individuals to evaluate "groupmates" more positively than "non-groupmates," even before they met them (Brewer, 1979; Gerard and Hoyt, 1974). Particularly as they enter adolescence, students seek an identity, a peer group with which to affiliate. In some cases, cross-racial friendships that existed in elementary school are broken in junior high, as students come to identify more with their own ethnic group. Cooperative learning provides each student with a group that is not based on racial or sexual identity, but on shared goals; the mere announcement of group assignments may begin to break down racial barriers to friendship as students perceive their shared identity.

A Model of Effects of Cooperative Learning on Intergroup Relations

The preceding section discusses the components of contact theory and of the cooperative learning methods in terms of their impact on intergroup relations. The research exploring the mechanisms by which cooperative learning might affect intergroup relations is sketchy at this point, although there is enough research to permit a preliminary discussion of a model linking the elements of cooperative learning to intergroup relations outcomes. A theoretical model of the effects of cooperative learning on intergroup relations is depicted in Figure 4.1.

Note that in Figure 4.1, cooperative learning is broken down into three primary components that are usually seen together in practice but are distinct in theory. These are assignment to mixed-race groups, provision of group tasks, and setting of cooperative goals and rewards. As discussed earlier, the simple assignment of students to mixed race teams, even without contact, is likely to give students a new basis of similarity across race lines and to communicate an unmistakable institutional norm that interracial interaction is normal and desirable, both of which may increase cross-racial friendships independently of contact per se. Group tasks (which could of course be assigned without group assignments or cooperative goals) are hypothesized to operate primarily through interracial

FIGURE 4.1   Contact Theory Model of Effect of Cooperative Learning on Intergroup Relations

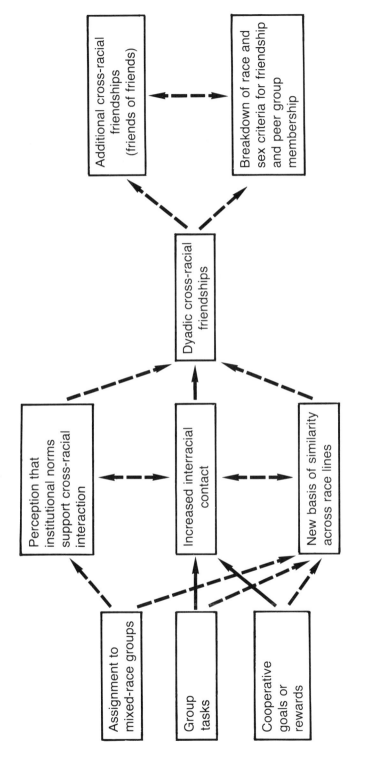

Established causal link
Hypothesized causal link

interaction (contact), although working on a group task may also provide students of different races with a new basis of similarity as well. However, the true effects of group tasks may depend on their particulars. For example, if students are allowed to choose partners to perform a task, they may choose within their own race groups, potentially reducing interracial interaction. If the task is such that interaction among many students is likely, and students of different races are likely to interact, the effect of the group task (through the increased contact) may be positive even without group assignment or cooperative goals. Cooperative goals and rewards are hypothesized to affect intergroup relations in part by increasing interracial interaction, in part by giving students a new basis of status similarity, but also in part directly, by creating a common, cooperative goal that is likely to increase mutual positive feelings among those who share the goal (see Johnson and Johnson, 1972).

However, note the centrality of interracial contact in the model depicted in Figure 4.1. In schools, where situational status differences are unlikely to exist between students in the same grade, non-superficial interracial contact is probably the critical mediating variable linking cooperative learning to improved intergroup relations. If cooperative learning did not create conditions of frequent positive, close interaction betweeen students of different races, whatever effects might be produced by assignment to groups or provision of cooperative goals and rewards might be weak and temporary. The various elements of cooperative learning probably affect interracial relations primarily through the mediating variable of close interracial contact.

One limitation of existing research on cooperative learning and on contact theory in general is the concentration of attention on dyadic relationships across race lines or (to a lesser extent) attitudes toward entire racial groups. However, the impact of cooperative learning almost certainly involves networks of friendships rather than simple dyadic friendships. New preliminary analyses of the data from the Slavin (1979) STAD study have revealed that many of the new cross-racial friendships made over the course of the STAD intervention were formed between students who had never been in the same cooperative group. A moment's reflection would support the inevitability of this result; in a four-member team that has two blacks and two whites, each student could only make two new friends of a different race if he or she made new friends only within the team. At least one of those teammates of a different race is also likely to be of a different sex; norms against black-white dating aside, cross-sex friendships are even less frequent than are cross-race friendships (Cooper et al., 1980; DeVries and Edwards, 1974). It is also possible that two or more teammates of different races were already friends, further restricting the possible number of new cross-racial, within team choices, and any deviation from a 50-50 racial split reduces the possibilities still further.

Apparently, cross-racial friendships formed outside of cooperative groups account for some of the effects of cooperative learning on dyadic interracial friendships. In theory, this should not happen; after all, the teams are usually in competition with each other. However, there are at least two ways this could happen. First, a cooperative learning experience often introduces students to their first (or best) cross-racial friendships. Racial groups in classrooms are characterized by many friendship ties within each race group but few outside of them. However, once a cross-racial friendship is formed, the new friend's friends (of his or her race) become likely candidates for friends as well. In other words, if a white student makes his or her first black friend, this relationship bridges formerly isolated black and white peer groups, and opens up an entirely new pool of potential black friends, even possibly reaching beyond the confines of a particular classroom. Also, even a small number of cross-racial friendships may make peer group boundaries, formerly based on race (and sex) criteria, less well-defined, allowing for new, smaller cliques to form based more on mutual liking than on race and sex. This pattern was found in the analysis of sociometric data conducted by Hansell, Tackaberry, and Slavin (1981); clique sizes tended to diminish as a result of a cooperative intervention similar to STAD.

Chapter Summary: Cooperative Learning and Intergroup Relations

The results of the studies relating cooperative learning to intergroup relations clearly indicate that when students work in ethnically mixed cooperative learning groups, they gain in cross-ethnic friendships. This research indicates that the effects of cooperative learning on intergroup relations are strong and long lasting, and are more likely to be seen on close, reciprocated friendship choices than on distant or unreciprocated choices. There are no clear patterns indicating more consistent results for some methods than others, as all methods have had some positive effects on intergroup relations.

The evidence discussed in this chapter generally supports Allport's (1954) contact theory. However, it raises some important questions about contact theory and related issues. The most important is whether contact per se is the critical variable in intergroup relations, instead of cooperative contact. One study (Cooper et al., 1980) found that contact in the form of competition between equals had as positive an effect on cross-race friendships as did cooperation. On the other hand, there is evidence that the greater the value of cooperative rewards, the more group cooperation improves intergroup relations. To the degree that it increases the value of cooperative rewards, use of group competition apparently increases the positive effect of cooperative learning on intergroup relations.

Allport (1954) emphasizes equality of status between individuals of different races as a precondition of positive relations between them. His reference was to situational status (Cook, 1969), by which definition all students in the same grade have the same status. However, Cohen (1975) has raised the issue of whether perceived (or actual) performance differences between students of different ethnicities will interfere with the development of positive relationships between them, and whether cooperative learning, by making performance differences more salient, will damage interethnic relations. Positive effects of the cooperative learning methods on intergroup relations provide little support for Cohen's concerns, supporting instead Allport's (1954) focus on situational rather than performance or ability status.

It is suggested that the fact of assigning students to ethnically heterogeneous groups communicates institutional norms favoring interethnic mixing, and creates a new basis of perceived similarity. However, classroom research has not separately addressed these issues.

The implications of the research reported in this chapter for practice are unambiguous; there is a strong positive effect of cooperative learning on intergroup relations. However, there is much work to be done to discover the critical components of cooperative learning for intergroup relations and to inform a model of how cooperative learning methods operate to affect intergroup relations.

5

Cooperative Learning and Mainstreaming of Academically Handicapped Students

In the 1940s and 50s, educators concerned with providing the best possible education for the child with learning problems advocated the development of special programs for these children which removed them from regular classrooms. Part of the impetus behind the effort to remove these children from the regular classrooms was that they were rejected by and isolated from other children in their classes because of their academic incompetence, and that this experience was harmful to their social development and their self-concept (Johnson, 1950; Shattuck, 1946). It was felt that removing the child from this hostile environment was essential to foster emotional and social development, as well as academic growth.

However, disappointing results of research on the academic and social outcomes of special class placement as well as concerns over the negative effects of segregating a child from normal-progress peers and other normal experiences that form a vital part of education (Dunn, 1968) promoted the development of the current policy of "mainstreaming." Within this system, now mandated by the Federal government under Public Law 94-142, children with mild academic handicaps in need of special education are placed in the "least restrictive environment" possible. By "mild academic handicaps" is meant academic performance that is significantly behind that of "normal-progress" students (usually at least two grade levels behind). Students with such mild academic handicaps are usually described as learning disabled or educable mentally retarded. These children are often placed in regular classes for the largest part of their school day, and given supportive educational services by a special teacher. Usually this requires that students go to resource rooms where they receive more individualized instruction for an hour or more a day.

Now that the academically handicapped child has been placed back in the regular classroom, research has again demonstrated poor relationships between special and regular class children. Students classified as learning disabled, who are of normal intelligence but not performing up to grade level expectations, have been studied in five studies (Bruininks, 1978; Bryan, 1974, 1976; Scranton and Ryckman, 1979; and Siperstein, Bop, and Bak, 1978). In each case, the learning disabled students were mainstreamed into regular classes for more than half of their school day, and the remainder of their day was spent in special programs. The findings of these studies were consistent in showing that learning disabled children in all elementary grades were less well accepted and more frequently rejected on sociometric instruments than were their normal-progress peers.

Similar results have been found in studies of mainstreamed educable mentally retarded students (Bruininks, Rynders, and Gross, 1974; Goodman, Gottlieb, and Harrison, 1972; Gottlieb, Semmel, and Veldman, 1979; Iano, Ayers, Heller, McGettigan, and Walker, 1974; Rucker, Howe, and Snider, 1969). Lapp (1957) found that in a program in which a small group of educable mentally retarded students was very carefully integrated into regular classes by specifically training teachers in strategies to deal with peer problems, the EMR students were still named as friends less often than their normal-progress peers, but they were no more rejected. This was in contrast to the other studies in which no particular strategies of mainstreaming were implemented and EMR or learning disabled students were always more rejected than were normal-progress students.

Thus, the finding of low social acceptance seems to be a stable one for mildly academically handicapped students, whether identified as educable mentally retarded or learning disabled. It appears that many factors may contribute to this finding of low status, including poor social skills leading to negative interaction (Bryan, 1974, 1976; Bruininks, 1978).

However, there is some evidence that while these factors appear to lead to poor acceptance and frequent rejection, the outcomes may be positively affected by particular classroom interventions. The study by Lapp (1957), in which no higher rejection was found for special students in a situation where integration was carefully programmed, suggests that structuring of the social situation can prevent the development of negative relationships. A few other researchers have evaluated classroom interventions specifically designed to improve the social status of academically handicapped students. All of these interventions have used some form of cooperative interaction between academically handicapped and normal-progress students to attempt to improve relationships between them. They draw on the same theories of cooperation and friendship formation on which the research on the effects of cooperative learning on race relations (Chapter 4) and general mutual attraction (Chapter 6) are based. However, they are not categorized as cooperative learning studies because their procedures and goals are only tangentially instructional. Chennault (1967) attempted to improve the social status of selected low status EMR students within the special class. Unpopular junior and senior high school special class children were paired with popular special class children, and then these pairs were taken out of the classroom for 15 minutes twice a week to plan, rehearse, and present a dramatic skit. The skit was presented to the class at the end of five weeks. A control group of low status students remained in the class. Social acceptance, as measured by a scale in which each student rated each other student on how much he or she wanted that student as a friend, improved for the students in the experimental group significantly more than for the control group. It would seem that the effect of this treatment would be to change the perception of the low status child by the child's classmates, perhaps by enabling the child to demonstrate competence in a special area and by pairing him or her with a high status child.

A replication of this study was conducted by Rucker and Vincenzo (1970). The same initial differences were found, but follow-up measures indicated that these gains had dissipated within one month after treatment. These researchers used a similar population, design, treatment and measures, with the exception that the pairs of students met for 45 minute sessions twice per week for only two weeks to plan a carnival rather than a skit for their classmates. A sociometric posttest was conducted three days after the carnival, and a follow-up test was conducted one month later. The gain in acceptance was seen for the low status students at the posttest, as in Chennault's study; at follow-up, however, there were no differences between the groups. The gains in status for the low acceptance students had dissipated once the treatment was discountinued.

Lilly (1971) studied a similar intervention to improve the social status of low achieving students (not identified as learning disabled or educable mentally retarded) within the regular classroom. He again paired popular and unpopular students, and removed them from the class for two fifteen minute periods a week for five weeks. During this time, the students made a movie which was presented to the class at the end of the project. Four other treatments, which isolated components of the full treatment, were also compared to a control group. In one of these, designed to evaluate the impact of the intervention of the experimenter leading the group, a student leader was selected to lead the group while the experimenter withdrew as much as was possible. In a treatment designed to isolate the effect of pairing low status children with popular peers, only low status children participated in the treatment. To assess the effect of removing the students from the class during the regular school day, one group met on a Saturday rather than during the week. To determine the impact of conducting a treatment outside of the classroom rather than inside, one group was assigned to complete a project in class rather than outside of the class. Lilly's findings showed significantly greater improvement in peer acceptance for all of the treatment groups, analyzed as a group, as compared to the control group. No single treatment group, even the full program, was found to be superior to the others. This suggests that simply involving the child in a special activity is the factor operating to improve the social status of these low status children in this study. However, the importance of this finding is diminished by the results of the follow-up conducted six to seven weeks after the end of the intervention. Again, gains were not maintained; there were no differences between the treatment and control groups at follow-up. It would thus appear that short term, high intensity interventions may not be effective in producing a lasting change in the social status of low status students.

A few studies have demonstrated that cooperative interventions involving academically handicapped and normal-progress students outside of the school setting can increase positive interactions between them. Martino and Johnson (1979) studied a summer swimming program. They assigned some students to pairs of learning disabled and normal-progress students, and they assigned others to swim individually. The frequency of friendly interactions between the learning disabled and normal-progress students was much higher in the "pairs" condition than in the individual swimming condition, and hostile interactions were less frequent. Johnson, Rynders, Johnson, Schmidt, and Haider (1980) compared cooperative, individualistic, and laizzez-faire interventions in bowling activities involving normal-progress and retarded (high-trainable) adolescents. Again, more friendly interactions between normal-progress and retarded students were seen, although there were no differences in negative (hostile) interactions.

In a similar study, Rynders, Johnson, Johnson, and Schmidt (1980) found more positive interactions between non-handicapped and Down's syndrome students in cooperative bowling groups than in competitive or individualistic ones. Non-handicapped students in the cooperative conditions also ranked the Down's syndrome students marginally ($p < .10$) higher as students with whom they would most like to bowl than they did in the competitive and individualistic conditions, and the Down's syndrome students ranked the non-handicapped students higher in the cooperative than in the competitive or individualistic conditions. A separate analysis from the same study (Johnson, Johnson, and Rynders, 1981) also found that students in the cooperative condition felt they were better bowlers than did students in the competitive or individualistic conditions.

The bowling and swimming studies are interesting as demonstrations, but because they measured interactions (and, in one case, rankings) that have meaning only in the context of the settings and interventions, their relevance to academic mainstreaming or to changing attitudes toward the handicapped is limited.

Cooperative Learning as a Potential Solution

The repeated failures to find long-lasting effects of special short-term cooperative classroom interventions designed to improve the status of the mainstreamed children suggest that cooperative learning programs that are designed for indefinite use may be required to fundamentally change the acceptance of these children. There is good reason to believe that the structure of the traditional classroom contributes to negative affect expressed toward low-performing students. Students in almost all classrooms are in competition with one another for acceptable grades and other rewards (Johnson and Johnson, 1974; Slavin, 1977a). Only a few, those who do *better* than the others, will receive "A's." The academically handicapped special child, who is inevitably on the "losing" end of the competition more frequently than on the "winning" side, is no doubt an appropriate target for expression of the negative feelings found to be generated in competitive situations.

A study of childrens' attitudes concerning the extent to which another child deserved a reward under a competitive reward structure showed that children who were unsuccessful under competitive conditions were seen as less deserving of rewards by those who were successful. Under noncompetitive conditions, no such differences were observed (Ames, Ames, and Felker, 1977). The deprecating comments common in competitive situations (Stendler et al., 1951) could thus be expected to fall upon the special child more frequently than on other, more academically competent children. Growth of friendship and acceptance is unlikely in this situation. The findings of Rucker and Vincenzo (1970) and Lilly (1971), that gains in sociometric status for low status children were not maintained after the brief cooperative intervention designed to improve status was completed, should not be surprising when examined in light of an understanding of the usual competitive structure of the classroom.

The interventions designed to increase the social status of low status mainstreamed children have involved short term interventions intended to boost the status of these children. They have operated on the assumption that once the child's status is improved, social forces will maintain the improvement. Since it seems unlikely, given the competitive structure of the traditional classroom, that this assumption is tenable, a cooperative intervention that changes this structure and can be imbedded in the ongoing classroom system may be required to bring about lasting improvement in the social status of mainstreamed children.

The cooperative learning methods described in this book are an obvious means of introducing cooperative activities into the ongoing instructional program in such a way as to accomplish the goals of mainstreaming while also accomplishing the basic instructional goals of schooling. The positive effects of cooperative learning on interpersonal relations, especially race relations (Chapter 4), suggest that cooperative learning programs may be able to overcome the barrier to friendship and acceptance created by differences between academically handicapped and normal-progress students. Differences in academic competence may provide a status barrier to contact between mainstreamed and normal-progress students, perhaps similar to that imposed by race. In addition, poor social and communication skills (Bryan, 1974, 1976) of academically handicapped students may discourage normal-progress students from pursuing relationships with these children. In the cooperative learning group, academic status is no longer the most important determinant of status, as group membership becomes more important and all students can participate as members of the group. Within the structure of the cooperative group, each student is a full member of the group, regardless of academic ability, and thus contact is in one sense on an equal status basis. The opportunity and necessity for cooperative helping interactions requires that students overcome the poor social skills and other problems of academically handicapped students in order to facilitate the success of the group. More positive contact is required, which should foster positive interactions leading to friendship.

RESEARCH ON COOPERATIVE LEARNING
AND MAINSTREAMING

At present, ten studies have been conducted to evaluate cooperative learning methods in mainstreamed classrooms. Nine of these involved three of the principal cooperative learning methods emphasized in this book: STAD, TAI, and Learning Together. The tenth (Ballard, Corman, Gottlieb, and Kaufman, 1977) is a study specifically directed at improving attitudes of normal-progress students toward academically handicapped classrooms that is more in the tradition of the Chennault (1967), Lilly (1971), and Rucker and Vincenzo (1970) studies described earlier than in the cooperative learning tradition. However, the Ballard et al. study took place over a much longer period than the other interventions (40 minutes per day for eight weeks), involved entire classes instead of special project groups, and was constructed around an instructional activity instead of a project outside of the classroom. For these reasons, the Ballard et al. (1977) study was considered as part of the cooperative learning field experimental research emphasized in this book.

Table 5.1 summarizes the characteristics and outcomes of the research on cooperative learning and acceptance of academically handicapped students. The studies presented in Table 5.1 are all methodologically adequate studies of cooperative learning of at least two weeks' duration involving academically or emotionally handicapped students in regular classes. As in Tables 3.2 and 4.1, a "+" indicates a statistically significant ($p<.05$) difference in favor of a cooperative condition on the indicated measure. A "(+)" indicates a marginally significant effect ($p<.10$), and a "0" indicates no significant differences. Some of the Learning Together studies used one-tailed t-tests. Since most of the cooperative learning studies used F's (equivalent to two-tailed t-tests), these one-tailed tests cannot

TABLE 5.1 Characteristics and Cross-Handicap Relations Outcomes of Cooperative Learning Field Experiments

Major Reports	Number of Students	Grade Level	Duration (Weeks)	Level of Random Assignment	Kind of School	Handicap Composition	Type of Measure	Cross-Handicap Relations Effects
Student Teams-Achievement Divisions (STAD)								
Madden and Slavin, in press	183	3–6	6	Class	Urban East	AH-22%	Sociometric Friendship	0
							Sociometric Rejection	+
Team Assisted Individualization (TAI)								
Slavin, Madden, and Leavy, 1982	286	3–5	8	School	Suburban East	AH-9%	Sociometric Friendship	+
							Sociometric Rejection	+
Learning Together								
Cooper, Johnson, Johnson, and Wilderson, 1980	57	7	3	Student	Urban Midwest	LD or ED-20%	Sociometric Friendship	+
					Suburban Midwest		Sociometric	
Armstrong, Johnson, and Balow, 1981	40	5–6	4	Student	Suburban Midwest	LD-25%	Sociometric Friendship	0
D. W. Johnson and R. T. Johnson, in press	51	4	3	Student	Suburban Midwest	LD or ED-24%	Free Time Interaction	0
							Handicapped Participation	0
R. T. Johnson and D. W. Johnson, in press a	40	3	3	Student	Suburban Midwest	LD or ED-20%	Sociometric Friendship	0
							Free Time Interaction	+

TABLE 5.1 (continued)

Major Reports	Number of Students	Grade Level	Duration (Weeks)	Level of Random Assignment	Kind of School	Handicap Composition	Type of Measure	Cross-Handicap Relations Effects
R. T. Johnson and D. W. Johnson, in press b	51	4	3	Student	Suburban Midwest	LD or ED-20%	Free Time Interaction	(+)
R. T. Johnson and D. W. Johnson, in press c	59	4	3	Student	Suburban Midwest	LD or ED-20%	Free Time Interaction	0
D. W. Johnson and R. T. Johnson, 1981c	31	11	3	Student	Suburban Midwest	LD or ED-10% EMR-10%	Sociometric Friendship	+
Ballard et al. Study Ballard, Corman, Gottlieb, and Kaufman, 1977	37 classes	3–5	8	Class	Urban Texas	1 EMR/ class	Sociometric Friendship Sociometric Rejection	+ 0

+   Cooperative learning group exceeded control group significantly ($p<.05$)
(+)   Cooperative group exceeded control group marginally ($p<.10$)
AH   Academically handicapped (learning disabled or EMR)
LD   Learning disabled
ED   Emotionally disturbed or disruptive
EMR   Educable mentally retarded

be compared to the more conservative F statistics. For this reason, results for one-tailed tests are presented as though two-tailed tests (or F's) had been used.

Two principal types of measures have been used to study the effects of cooperative learning on cross-handicap relations: sociometric and observational. Many studies used sociometric friendship measures, such as "Who are your friends in this class?" and a few used sociometric rejection measures, such as "If you were going to be working on a project with other children, there might be some children you would *not* want to have in your group. Please name these children if there are any." Only the Learning Together studies used observational measures of cross-handicap interaction. In general, they provided a ten-minute free period at the end of class, and observed the frequency of cross-handicap interactions in experimental and control classes. As noted in Chapter 4, this measure of interaction may not have meaning outside of the classroom setting, as students may simply stay in their heterogeneous groups during the free time, but these studies are important in actually observing cross-handicap interaction instead of depending only on paper-and-pencil sociometric measures. Many studies reported such measures as "Who has helped you in this class?" and in-class observations of interaction between academically handicapped and normal-progress classes. Since cross-handicap interactions are mandated by the cooperative treatments, these findings are not presented as outcomes of the treatments.

One study of STAD (Madden and Slavin, in press) has been conducted in mainstreamed classes. In this study, academically handicapped students received many fewer rejection choices in the STAD groups than in control groups, controlling for pretests. However, there were no differences on a sociometric "friends" measure. TAI was specifically developed (under funding from the U.S. Office of Special Education) to solve the problems of the mainstreamed classroom, and as a consequence, the effects of TAI on cross-handicap acceptance and other variables were stronger than those for STAD (Slavin, Madden, and Leavey, 1982). Positive effects were found both for sociometric friendships toward academically handicapped students and for reducing the frequency with which academically handicapped students were nominated neither as "friends" nor as "OK." Further, marked improvements were seen in teacher ratings of the academically handicapped students' behavior. On four scales, classroom behavior, self-confidence, friendship behavior, and negative peer behavior, the TAI classes were rated as having many fewer problems, controlling for pretests. In fact, by the time of the posttest, academically handicapped students in the TAI classes were rated as equal in behavior problems to normal-progress students in the control classes, even though they had been rated much worse than these students on the pretests.

Seven of the ten cooperative learning studies involving mainstreaming of academically handicapped students evaluated the effects of the Learning

Together model on cross-handicap relations. These studies are very similar to one another. They all used random assignment of students, very small sample sizes (the largest sample is 59 students), and brief durations (4 weeks). They all used the same cooperative treatment, in which students work in small, heterogeneous groups to produce a single worksheet, and are praised and rewarded as a group (but "praise and rewards" are informal, not based on members' learning or the quality of the group product). Four of the studies used the free time observation measures described above, and sociometric "friends" measures are reported in one of these and in the remaining three studies.

The results of the Learning Together studies on acceptance of academically and emotionally handicapped students are inconsistent, but generally positive. Cooper, Johnson, Johnson, and Wilderson (1980) found significantly more friendship choices directed at academically or emotionally handicapped students in a cooperative condition than in an individualistic one, but there were no differences between the cooperative condition and a competitive one. Armstrong, Johnson, and Balow (1981) found no difference between cooperative and individualistic treatments on sociometric measures. They did find positive effects on two peer rating scales, on which students rated one another from smart to dumb and from valuable to worthless, but there was no separate analysis of ratings of the academically handicapped students.

One of the four studies that measured cross-handicap interaction during free time found significantly positive effects for the cooperative treatment (R. T. Johnson and D. W. Johnson, in press a), and one additional study (R. T. Johnson and D. W. Johnson, in press b) found marginally significant positive effects. The remaining two studies (D. W. Johnson and R. T. Johnson, in press; R. T. Johnson and D. W. Johnson, in press c) found no differences. The D. W. Johnson and R. T. Johnson (in press) study used a measure in which students were assigned to new groups and asked to play a structured game, to determine whether or not a tendency toward cross-handicap interaction would transfer to a new setting and task. No differences were found, although the trend favored the cooperative treatments.

Finally, D. W. Johnson and R. T. Johnson (1980) found more cross-handicap acceptance as a work partner in a cooperative condition than in an individualistic one, although it is not stated whether positive effects were found both for acceptance of handicapped students by their peers and for acceptance of non-handicapped students by handicapped classmates.

The earliest and largest of the cooperative learning field experiments to study the effects of cooperation in heterogeneous groups on acceptance of academically handicapped students was conducted by Ballard, Corman, Gottlieb, and Kaufman (1977). In this study, thirty-seven classes in grades 3-5 were randomly assigned to cooperative or control conditions (25 experimental, 12 control). One EMR student was in each class. In the cooperative classes, students were assigned to 4-6 member heterogeneous groups; one group in each class contained the EMR student. The groups worked together to plan, produce, and present a multimedia project. Students were instructed to break their task down into subtasks to be performed by each group member. The results indicated that EMR's in the experimental groups were better accepted by their classmates than were control EMR's, controlling for pretests. There were no differences in sociometric rejections.

Studies in Self-Contained Special Classrooms. One issue related to cooperative learning and mainstreaming is the use of cooperative learning methods in special schools for emotionally disturbed adolescents. Two studies have evaluated TGT in such settings.

Slavin (1977d) compared TGT to a control group in two classes in a middle school for emotionally disturbed students of normal intelligence. Students were randomly assigned to classes, and both classes were taught by the same pair of teachers. Social studies achievement, in-class observations, and sociometric questions served as the dependent measures with respective pretests as covariates.

The results indicated no achievement differences, but the TGT students were on-task significantly more than control students. They also named significantly more of their classmates as friends and desired workmates. Five months after the conclusion of the study, when students had been reassigned to new classes, follow-up behavior observations indicated that former TGT students interacted with their peers significantly more than did former control students. As appropriate peer interaction was a major goal of the special program, this was seen as a particularly important finding.

Janke (1978) replicated the Slavin (1977d) study in three schools for high school aged emotionally disturbed students. Students were randomly assigned to three classrooms in each of three schools. Two of the classrooms in each school experienced TGT, while the third served as a control group. The Janke (1978) study was the longest of the TGT studies; students were in their treatments for eighteen weeks. The subject matter was mathematics.

The results of the Janke (1978) study, as for the Slavin (1977d) study, indicated no achievement differences but higher time on-task for the TGT classes. Behavioral observations also indicated less disruptive behavior in the TGT classes than in control, and higher daily attendance in the TGT classes.

Thus, the Slavin (1977d) and Janke (1978) studies are consistent in indicating that TGT can improve the behavior of emotionally disturbed adolescents in self-contained classes but not their achievement.

Conclusions: Cooperative Learning and Mainstreaming

The research on cooperative learning and relationships between academically handicapped and normal-progress students generally shows that cooperative learning can overcome this barrier to friendship and interaction. Further, in the cases of the Madden and Slavin (in press) and Slavin, Madden, and Leavey (1982) studies, these improvements can be obtained at the same time as achievement is enhanced for all students in the class. These studies did not find significantly greater achievement for academically handicapped students in the cooperative classes, although this may be due to the small numbers of academically handicapped students involved; in both studies, the academically handicapped students in the experimental groups out-performed those in the control groups by a larger amount than normal-progress students in experimental groups exceeded those in control groups (for whom the differences were statistically significant). The practical importance of these findings is that schools can meet the academic and social needs of their academically handicapped students while enhancing the academic achievement of their normal-progress students. This is critical; few schools would use a program designed to aid mainstreamed students if it did not also improve (or at least not retard) the achievement of the rest of the class.

While the research on cooperative learning and mainstreaming is promising, it is still at a somewhat early stage relative to the research reported earlier on student achievement (Chapter 3) and intergroup relations (Chapter 4). Positive effects on cross-handicap relations are found less consistently than are effects on intergroup relations. Further, serious problems of generalizability from the immediate setting of the experiment are present in many of the studies discussed in this chapter. None of the studies use long-term follow-ups of sociometric findings or out-of-class observations to determine whether or not in-class observations have external validity. The advantage of the cooperative learning methods is that because they are alternative forms of basic instruction, they can be used indefinitely, so the burden of long-term maintenance is not as heavy as it would be on a one-time "treatment." However, the studies by Rucker and Vincenzo (1970) and Lilly (1971), in which positive effects on the acceptance of academically handicapped students brought about by cooperative methods failed to maintain on follow-up, indicate that long-term effects must be a concern in mainstreaming research.

Still, even in light of the shortcomings of the research done so far, the possibilities of cooperative learning for improving mainstreaming as an intervention are exciting. Even if specific effects on paper-and-pencil measures or behavioral observations could not be detected in some cases, the fact that academically handicapped students can work side by side with their normal-progress peers as full participants in class activities, is in itself a breakthrough in mainstreaming. All too often "mainstreaming" involves putting academically handicapped students in regular classrooms where their learning problems cause them to be re-segregated. If use of cooperative learning strategies in the mainstreamed classroom can make it possible for academically handicapped students to be truly integrated with their normal-progress classmates, this would represent an important step forward.

6

Cooperative Learning: Other Non-Cognitive Outcomes

The previous chapters have reviewed the field experimental evidence concerning the effects of cooperative learning methods on the three outcomes that have generated the greatest practical interest and use of these methods: academic achievement, intergroup relations, and mainstreaming-related outcomes. However, there is a wide range of other non-cognitive outcomes that have been measured in the cooperative learning research. Some of these, such as behavioral observations of time on-task and scales measuring peer norms concerning achievement and expectancy-related dimensions, are important in building models of how cooperative learning increases student achievement. Others, such as measures of mutual attractions, cooperativeness, liking of school, and self-esteem, are important socialization outcomes in their own rights.

Table 6.1 summarizes the characteristics and outcomes of the various cooperative learning studies on the most frequently measured non-cognitive variables (others are discussed in the text). A "+" in the table indicates a statistically significant ($p < .05$) difference in which a cooperative learning group exceeded a control group on the indicated measure. A "(+)" indicates a marginally significant difference ($p < .10$), a "0" indicates no differences, and a "−" indicates a statistically significant difference favoring the control group. Even more than in previous chapters, the table should be interpreted only in the light of the text, as differences in measurement between the various studies are especially important for the non-cognitive outcomes.

Self-Esteem

Perhaps the most important psychological outcome of cooperative learning methods is their effect on student self-esteem. In one sense, the value of increasing student achievement is as much as a concrete demonstration to the student that he or she can learn as it is the achievement itself. Students' beliefs that they are valuable and important individuals are

TABLE 6.1 Characteristics and Non-cognitive Outcomes of Cooperative Learning Field Experiments

	Characteristics						Outcomes						
Major Reports	No. of Students	Grade Level	Duration (Weeks)	Level of Random Assignment	Kind of School		Self-Esteem	Pro-Academic Norms	Locus of Control	Time on Task	Liking of Class	Liking of Classmates	Cooperation
Student Teams Achievement Divisions (STAD)													
					Group Study, Group Reward for Learning Studies								
Slavin, 1978c	205	7	10	Class	Eastern Rural Town			+	+	+	0	+	
Slavin and Wodarski, 1978; Slavin, 1980a	424	4	12	Class	Rural East			0		+	0		
Oickle, 1980	1029	6–8	12	Class	Rural East		+	+			0	+	
Madden and Slavin, in press	175	3–6	6	Class	Urban East		+	+	+		0	+	
Allen and Van Sickle, 1981	51	9	6	Class	Rural South		0						
Sharan, Raviv, and Kussell, 1982	264	7	16	Teacher	Urban Israel								+
Teams-Games-Tournament (TGT)													
Edwards and DeVries, 1972; DeVries and Edwards, 1973	117	7	4	Student	Urban East						+	+	
Edwards and DeVries, 1974	128	7	12	Student	Urban East			+			+	+	

TABLE 6.1 (continued)

	Characteristics					Outcomes						
Major Reports	No. of Students	Grade Level	Duration (weeks)	Level of Random Assignment	Kind of School	Self-Esteem	Pro-Academic Norms	Locus of Control	Time on Task	Liking of Class	Liking of Classmates	Cooperation
Hulten and DeVries, 1976; Slavin, DeVries, and Hulten 1975	299	7	10	Class	Urban East		+			0		
DeVries, Edwards, and Wells, 1974b	191	10–12	12	Class	Suburban South			+		+	+	
DeVries and Mescon, 1975	60	3	6	Student	Suburban East		0			0	0	
DeVries, Mescon and Shackman, 1975b	53	3	6	Student	Suburban East		0			0	0	
DeVries, Lucasse, and Shackman, 1979	1742	7–8	10	Teacher	Suburban Midwest	+	0					
Slavin, 1975, 1977d	57	7–9	10	Class	Suburban East (Emotionally Disturbed)		+		+		+	

Study	N	Grade	Weeks	Assignment	Location							
Janke, 1978	90	8–10	18	Student	Urban Midwest (Emotionally Disturbed)				+	0		
Combined Student Team Learning Program												
Slavin and Karweit, 1981	559	4–5	16	Non-Random (Matched)	Rural East	+	0	0		+	+	
Team Assisted Individualization (TAI)												
Slavin, Leavey, and Madden, 1982												
Experiment 1	506	3–5	8	School	Suburban East	+			+	+	+	
Experiment 2	320	4–6	10	Non-Random (Matched)	Suburban East	+			0	0	+	
Other Group Study, Group Reward for Learning Studies												
Humphreys, Johnson, and Johnson, 1982 (Learning Together with Group Reward for Learning)	44	9	6	Student	Suburban Midwest					+		
Group Case Studies												
Learning Together												
Johnson, Johnson, Johnson, and Anderson, 1976	30	5	4	Student	Urban Midwest	+				+	+	+

TABLE 6.1 (continued)

| | Characteristics | | | | | Outcomes | | | | | | |
Major Reports	No. of Students	Grade Level	Duration (weeks)	Level of Random Assignment	Kind of School	Self-Esteem	Pro-Academic Norms	Locus of Control	Time on Task	Liking of Class	Liking of Classmates	Cooperation
Johnson, Johnson, and Scott, 1978	30	5–6	10	Student	Suburban Midwest	+		+				
Cooper et al., 1980	57	7	3	Student	Urban Midwest						+	
Johnson, and Johnson, 1981; D. W. Johnson and R. T. Johnson, in press	51	4	3	Student	Urban Midwest				+		(+)	
R. T. Johnson and D. W. Johnson, in press (a)	40	3	3	Student	Suburban Midwest				0			
R. T. Johnson and D. W. Johnson, in press (b)	51	4	3	Student	Suburban Midwest				0		+	
R.T. Johnson and D. W. Johnson, in press (c)	59	4	3	Student	Suburban Midwest	+						

Other Group Study Studies											
Wheeler and Ryan, 1973	88	5–6	4	Student	Suburban Midwest				+		
Starr and Schuerman, 1974	48	7	3	Class	Suburban Midwest				–		
Task Specialization, Group Reward for Learning Methods											
Jigsaw II											
Ziegler, 1981	146	6	8	Class	Urban Canada			+			
Task Specialization Methods											
Jigsaw											
Blaney, Stephan, Rosenfield, Aronson, and Sikes, 1977	304	5	6	Non-Random (matched)	Urban Southwest	+			0	0	+
Geffner, 1978	218	5	8	Non-Random (matched)	Rural California Town	+					
Gonzales, 1979	326	9–12	10	Non-Random (matched)	Rural California Town	0	+		0		
Gonzales, 1981	182	3–4	20	Non-Random (matched)	Rural California (Bilingual Classes)	0					0
Lazarowitz, Baird, Bowlden, and Hertz-Lazarowitz, 1982	109	10–12	6	Non-Random (matched)	Western Rural Town	+			+	(+)	+

TABLE 6.1 (continued)

	Characteristics						Outcomes						
Major Reports	No. of Students	Grade Level	Duration (Weeks)	Level of Random Assignment	Kind of School	Self-Esteem	Pro-Academic Norms	Locus of Control	Time on Task	Liking of Class	Liking of Classmates	Cooperation
Hertz-Lazarowitz, Sapir, and Sharan, 1982	71	8	5	Non-Random (matched)	Urban Israel							0
Group-Investigation												
Hertz-Lazarowitz, Sharan, and Steinberg, 1980	393	3–7	54	Non-Random (matched)	Urban Israel							+
Sharan, Raviv, and Kussell, 1982	234	7	16	Teacher	Urban Israel							+
Hertz-Lazarowitz, Sapir, and Sharan, 1982	67	8	5	Non-Random (matched)	Urban Israel							+
Other Task Specialization Studies												
Wheeler, 1977	40	5–6	3	Class	Southern Rural Town						+	

* Cooperative Learning group exceeded control group significantly ($p < .05$).
(+) Cooperative Learning group exceeded control group marginally significantly ($p < .10$).
0 No significant differences.
– Control group exceeded Cooperative Learning group significantly ($p < .05$).
Note: Please see text for explanations of findings.

of critical importance for their ability to withstand the disappointments of life, to be confident decision makers, and ultimately to be happy and productive individuals.

In a way, it hardly seems likely that a cooperative learning experience, typically in one class for a few weeks, would change student self-esteem. On the other hand, two of the most important components of students' self-esteem are the feeling that they are well liked by their peers and that they are doing well academically (see Chapter 1). Cooperative learning methods impact on both of these components. As a result of cooperative learning interventions, students are typically named as friends by more of their classmates, feel more successful in their academic work, and in fact achieve more than in traditional classrooms. For these reasons, it may be that an experience of cooperative learning would in fact increase students' self-esteem.

The evidence from the cooperative learning studies tends to bear this out, although there are many inconsistencies. The technique whose structure is most directly targetted to improving student self-esteem is Jigsaw, in which students are made to feel important because they have indispensible information that makes their contribution to the group critical. Blaney et al. (1977), Geffner (1978) and Lazarowitz, Baird, Bowlden, and Hertz-Lazarowitz (1982), found positive effects of Jigsaw on student self-esteem, although no differences were found in two studies by Gonzales (1979, 1981).

The STAD and TGT studies have often used modifications of the Coopersmith Self-Esteem Inventory (Coopersmith, 1967) to study the effects of these methods on student self-esteem. The Coopersmith scales used in this research are General Self-Esteem, Social Self-Esteem, and Academic Self-Esteem. Madden and Slavin (in press) found significantly greater general self-esteem in STAD than in control groups, controlling for pretests, but they found no differences on academic or social self-esteem. Oickle (1980) found positive effects of STAD on student self-esteem using the Piers-Harris Children's Self-Concept Scale, but Allen and Van Sickle (1981) found no differences for STAD on this variable. DeVries, Lucasse, and Shackman (1979) found that TGT increased students' social self-esteem but not their academic self-esteem. In the study combining STAD, TGT, and Jigsaw II, Slavin and Karweit (1981) found greater general and academic self-esteem, but not social self-esteem, for the experimental group than for the control group. This study also found that students expressed less anxiety in the cooperative groups than in the control groups.

Because of its use of individualized instruction, where students can be successful working at their own levels, TAI was expected to have especially strong effects on students' self-concepts in mathematics. Large effects on a questionnaire measure of self-concept in mathematics were found in Experiment 1 but not Experiment 2 (Slavin, Leavey, and Madden, 1982).

Another measure of self-esteem used in the TAI studies was teacher ratings of student self-esteem behaviors. Teachers rated a subsample of their students on such items as "(student) is extremely critical of himself/herself," "(student) lacks conficence," and "(student) quits when tasks become difficult." Teachers rated students on a scale from 0 (not a problem) to 4 (extremely serious problem). Controlling for pretests, teacher ratings of students' self-concepts were significantly higher in the TAI classes than in control in both of the TAI studies (Slavin, Leavey, and Madden, 1982).

Two of the Learning Together studies evaluated elements of self-esteem. Johnson, Johnson, and Scott (1978) found that students who had worked in groups were more likely than individualistically-taught students to agree that "I'm doing a good job of learning." R. T. Johnson and D. W. Johnson (in press c) found that cooperation increased students' general and school self-esteem more than competition or individualization, but they found no differences on peer self-esteem.

Thus the evidence concerning cooperative learning and self-esteem is not completely consistent, although it should be noted that in eleven of the fourteen studies in which the effects of cooperative learning on self-esteem were studied, positive effects on some aspect of self-esteem were found. This is a considerably higher success rate than was seen for liking of class (discussed later in this chapter), an outcome that should in theory be easier to change. The effects of cooperative learning on student self-esteem are probably short-lived and specific to the settings in which they were obtained; it is difficult to imagine a dramatic change in such a central part of students' psychological makeup from an intervention of a few weeks' duration. However, these results do suggest that if cooperative learning methods were used over longer periods as a principal instructional methodology, real and lasting changes in student self-esteem might be brought about.

Pro-Academic Peer Norms

The central mediating variable linking cooperative incentive structures to individual achievement is their presumed effect on peer norms concerning groupmates' achievement. This is discussed in detail in Chapters 1 and 3. Essentially, the argument is that cooperative incentives motivate students to try to get each other to do academic work, and by the same process get students to feel that their classmates want them to do their best. These normative forces, or interpersonal sanctions, have been found in studies outside of the cooperative learning tradition to be powerful influences on student achievement (Coleman, 1961; Brookover, Beady, Flood, Schweitzer, and Wisenbaker, 1979). It seems likely that if the peer group could be enlisted to encourage achievement, then achievement should increase.

Early laboratory research demonstrated that norms can be changed by the use of cooperative incentive structures. Deutsch (1949a) found that college students who discussed human relations problems under cooperative conditions felt more pressure to achieve from their groupmates, felt more of an obligation to their groupmates, and had a stronger desire to win their groupmates' respect than did students who worked under competitive instructions. These results taken together indicate that in the cooperative groups, students wanted to achieve because their groupmates wanted them to do so. Thomas (1975) found that individuals in cooperative groups exerted social pressures on one another to achieve. He called these "responsibility forces," interpersonal sanctions that maintain behavior that helps the group to succeed.

The field experimental research also supports the findings of effects of cooperative learning on peer norms supporting individual achievement. Four STAD studies found such effects. Slavin (1978c) found positive effects of STAD on a questionnaire scale consisting of such items as "students in this class want me to come to school every day," and "other students want me to work hard in this class." Madden and Slavin (in press) and Oickle (1980) also found positive effects of STAD on similar scales. Hulten and DeVries (1976) and Edwards and DeVries (1974) found similar results for TGT, although a few studies found no differences (DeVries and Mescon, 1975; DeVries, Mescon and Shackman, 1975b; Slavin and Karweit, 1981).

In addition to this direct evidence for effects of cooperative learning methods on student support for academic performance, there is some interesting indirect evidence. In a secondary analysis of data from the Hulten and DeVries (1976) TGT study, Slavin, DeVries, and Hulten (1975) found that academic success had positive social consequences for a student in a condition that used cooperative teams and competitive games, but negative consequences in a condition in which there were competitive games but no cooperative teams. It is important to note that due to the structure of the academic games, high achieving students had no particular advantage; success depended primarily on effort. Even so, the correlation between academic success (in the games) and gain in sociometric standing was significantly higher in the classes with cooperative teams than in the classes without them. This was replicated in a study of TGT in social studies classes in a middle school for emotionally disturbed adolescents (Slavin, 1975). In this study, there was a positive correlation between actual gains in academic achievement and improvement in sociometric status in the experimental group, while there was a negative correlation in the control group, suggesting that doing well academically was a socially approved activity in the cooperative learning class, while it was not in the control class.

One more indication of the effects of cooperative learning on peer support for academic achievement is that in two studies, the TGT study by Hulten and DeVries (1976) and a STAD study by Slavin (1980c), it was found that the positive effects of cooperative learning methods on academic achievement were due to the use of the cooperative reward system, not to students' chances to work together. Both studies employed control groups in which every detail of the implementation was identical to the experimental group except for the cooperative reward system and/or the group task. The cooperative reward system increased academic achievement even when students were forbidden to work together. Unless the students in both studies were somehow able to work together outside of class, the most plausible explanation for this finding is that the cooperative reward system created a condition in which interpersonal sanctions are exerted to get students to do well academically.

The evidence is not entirely unambiguous. First, it is possible that the questionnaire scales measuring peer norms are in fact just asking students to report what treatments they are in. For example, if a student reports that "my classmates care how I do in this class," he may simply be saying that they have a reason to care because they are on a team together, not that they really care. One study that measured peer support for achievement (Johnson and Johnson, 1981) was not included in Table 6.1 because the measure was too heavily biased toward the cooperative group (e.g. "other students like to help me learn"); since helping was discouraged in the individualistic control group, this could only be agreed with in the cooperative group. Also, one TGT study (DeVries, Lucasse, and Shackman, 1979), one STAD study (Slavin, 1979), and the study in which TGT, STAD and Jigsaw II were combined (Slavin and Karweit, 1981) failed to find effects of cooperative learning on questionnaire measures of peer support for academic performance. However, in no case have there been greater improvements on this variable in a control group than in an experimental group.

Locus of Control

The degree to which students believe that their academic success is dependent on their own efforts (internal locus of control) has been shown on many occasions to be the single personality variable most consistently related to high academic performance, controlling for such background factors as socioeconomic status (see, for example, Brookover et al., 1979; Coleman et al., 1966). Attribution theory (Weiner, 1979; Weiner and Kukla, 1970) also predicts that individuals who perceive their successes or failures to be due to unchangable features of themselves or their environments have less motivation and achieve less than students who feel that success or failure are due to their own efforts.

Cooperative learning might be hypothesized to influence locus of control for several reasons. The most obvious is that the cooperative learning methods tend to increase students' actual success, and individuals who experience success are much more likely than those who do not to believe that their efforts made the difference (Weiner and Kukla, 1970). In the Student Team Learning methods, the use of equal opportunity scoring systems is specifically designed to reward students for additional effort, regardless of ability, and this should produce a (correct) perception that outcomes depend on academic efforts. DuCette (1979) has pointed out that for high internal locus of control to exist and then to actually affect student achievement, effort must in fact lead to academic success, and academic success must be valued by the student. Particularly in the Student Team Learning methods, the connection between effort and academic success is clear, and in all of the cooperative learning methods, peer support for academic performance engendered by the cooperative incentive structure (see the previous section) increases the value to students of doing well academically.

Several of the cooperative learning studies have found that internal locus of control is positively influenced by these methods. Slavin (1978c) found that STAD increased students' feelings that their outcomes depended on their performance, rather than on luck, and DeVries, Edwards, and Wells (1974a) found similar effects for TGT. Gonzales (1979) found a positive effect of Jigsaw on internal locus of control. Johnson, Johnson, and Scott (1978) found that students who experienced the Learning Together model were less likely than control students to agree that "luck decides most things that happen to me," but they found no differences on the question, "If I work hard at something I will be good at it." One study found no differences on locus of control; the Slavin and Karweit (1981) study of the combined use of STAD, TGT, and Jigsaw II found no differences on Clifford's (1976) Academic Achievement Accountability Scale, although there were some problems with ceiling effects in both experimental conditions.

Several other cooperative learning studies examined other motivation-related attitudes or perceptions. Slavin (1978c) found that students in STAD reported more motivation than did control students. Johnson, Johnson, Johnson, and Anderson (1976) reported that students who had participated in Learning Together groups were more intrinsically motivated and less extrinsically motivated than were individualistically taught students. Hulten and DeVries (1976) and DeVries, Edwards, and Wells (1974b) found that TGT students felt it was more important to do well in class than did control students, and Oickle (1980) found the same result for STAD. Slavin (1978c) found STAD students to feel they had a better chance to do well than did control students. Along the same lines, one study showed that TGT students found their classes less difficult than did control students (DeVries, Edwards, and Wells, 1974b), although several other studies of TGT failed to replicate this.

In sum, there is some evidence that cooperative learning methods make students feel that they have a chance to succeed, that their efforts will lead to success, and that success is a valued goal. These are the essential features predicting high achievement in many theories of achievement motivation, such as expectancy theory (Kukla, 1972) and attribution theory (Weiner, 1979). It is possible that these changes in achievement-related perceptions partly explain the positive achievement outcomes of cooperative learning reported in Chapter 3.

Time On-Task and Classroom Behavior

One behavioral indication of student motivational involvement is the proportion of their class time they spend on-task. Behavioral observers have been used in several cooperative learning studies to collect information on this measure. The element of time on-task observed in all of these studies is *engaged time* (see Karweit and Slavin, 1981), the proportion of time students are doing their assigned work within the time available for work (i.e. excluding non-instructional time). Typically, the observers have observed all students or a selected subset of students in a prescribed order, noting whether or not each student is attending to the assigned task. Interobserver reliabilities of 0.80 or more are usually established.

Cooperative learning is hypothesized to increase time on-task by engaging students' attention (because of the social nature of the task) and by increasing their motivation to master academic materials. Most studies that have measured time on-task have found higher proportions of engaged time for the cooperative learning students than for control students. This was found for STAD (Slavin, 1978c; 1980a), for TGT (Janke, 1978; Slavin, 1977d), and for Jigsaw II (Ziegler, 1981). The results for the Learning Together model have been less consistent. D. W. Johnson and R. T. Johnson (in press) found more time on-task in Learning Together than in individualistic methods, but R. T. Johnson and D. W. Johnson (in press a) and R. T. Johnson and D. W. Johnson (in press b) found no differences on this variable.

The two TAI studies (Slavin, Leavey, and Madden 1982) used teacher ratings of student classroom behavior. Teachers rated a subsample of their class on a classroom behavior scale consisting of such items as "(student) does not attend to work," and "(student) constantly demands teacher's attention." Teachers rated each student on a scale from 0 (not a problem) to 4 (extremely serious problem) at pre- and posttest. Results indicated significantly higher ratings (controlling for pretests) for the TAI students in Experiment 1, but there were no differences in Experiment 2.

Finally, attendance is a major determinant of students' ultimate time on-task. Janke (1978) found that TGT increased student attendance (compared to control groups) in a school for emotionally disturbed adolescents.

Liking of Class

Various questionnaire measures of liking of class, liking of school, or liking of the subject matter being taught have been administered in the course of the research on cooperative learning. The hypothesis that students would enjoy working cooperatively more than individualistically is almost obviously correct; anyone walking into a class using any of the cooperative learning methods can see that the students enjoy working with each other. When the students are asked if they liked working cooperatively and would like to do so again, they enthusiastically say that they would.

However, the research evidence on this variable is more equivocal than for any of the other non-cognitive outcomes. Some studies have found greater liking of class in cooperative than control classes (DeVries, Edwards, and Wells, 1974a; Edwards and DeVries, 1972, 1974; Humphreys et al., 1982; Johnson et al., 1976; Lazarowitz et al., 1982; Slavin and Karweit, 1981; Slavin, Leavey, and Madden, 1982 (Exp. 1); Wheeler and Ryan, 1973). However, about as many studies found no differences in liking of class between cooperative and control classes (e.g. Slavin and Wodarski, 1978; Slavin, 1978c; Madden and Slavin, in press; Oickle, 1980; DeVries, Mescon, and Shackman, 1975b; Hulten and DeVries, 1976; DeVries and Mescon, 1975; Slavin, Leavey, and Madden, 1980 (Exp. 2); Gonzales, 1979; Janke, 1978). Blaney et al. (1977) found that Anglos and blacks increased in liking of class more in Jigsaw than in control conditions, but Mexican-American students' liking of class increased more in the control group. Starr and Schuerman (1974) found that their control group gained more in liking of class than their experimental group. Hertz-Lazarowitz, Sapir, and Sharan (1981) found that students expressed a stronger preference for Group-Investigation than for Jigsaw.

One of the problems in measurement of liking of class is that most students, especially at the elementary level, tend to report on the pretest that they like class, so that the measurement on the posttest cannot discriminate students who like class more than they did before from those who like it the same as before. In the TGT studies that took place in third grades (DeVries and Mescon, 1975; DeVries, Mescon, and Shackman, 1975b), this is certainly part of the reason that no effects were found, as more than ninety percent of the students in both experimental conditions agreed that they liked class on the pre- and posttests. Similar ceiling effects may account for many or most of the failures to find significant differences. Also, when students were directly asked whether they liked the method they experienced (cooperative or control), they did express greater liking for the cooperative method (Johnson, Johnson, Johnson, and Anderson, 1976, Humphreys, Johnson, and Johnson, 1982; Madden and Slavin, in press). This implies that part of the failure to find significant differences on the more global "liking of class" measures could be due to the fact that students were not being asked to compare experiences with different methods but to give their general feelings about school.

Liking of Classmates and Feeling Liked by Classmates

Because cooperative learning methods are social interventions, they should produce social effects. The criteria for positive intergroup relations outlined by Allport (1954) are similar to the widely accepted antecedents of friendship formation or cohesion (see Lott and Lott, 1965). These include contact; perceived similarity; engaging in pleasant activities; and once again, cooperation, where individuals who work toward the same goal come to see one another as providers of rewards (see Deutsch, 1949b; Johnson and Johnson, 1972). Cooperative learning increases contact between students, gives them a shared basis of similarity (group membership), engages them in pleasant activities together, and has them work toward common goals. As such, it can clearly be hypothesized that they would increase positive affect between students.

Relationships between students have been measured in a variety of ways. In some studies, the number of names listed in response to a sociometric question such as "Who are your friends in this class?" is used as a measure of mutual attraction. Many studies use questionnaire scales with items such as "I like the other students in this class" and "the other students in this class like me."

Slavin (1978c) found positive effects of STAD on the number of friends named and on a "liking of others" questionnaire scale, but not on a "feeling of being liked" scale. Oickle (1980) also found positive effects of STAD on the number of students named as friends but not on questionnaire scales measuring liking of others or feelings of being liked. DeVries and Edwards (1973) found that TGT increased student scores on a mutual concern questionnaire scale, but not on a cohesiveness scale or on the number of friends named, while Edwards and DeVries (1974) found positive effects of TGT on mutual concern, cohesiveness, and number of friends named. Slavin (1977d) found that TGT increased the number of friends named in classes for emotionally disturbed adolescents.

In the combined study of STAD, TGT, and Jigsaw II, Slavin and Karweit (1981) found that the cooperative learning students named more friends than did control students, and they named fewer classmates as individuals with whom they would not like to work. However, there were no treatment differences on questionnaire scales measuring liking of classmates or feelings of being liked. In the two TAI studies (Slavin, Leavey, and Madden, 1982), teachers rated a subsample of their students on friendship-related problems (e.g., "(student) has few or no friends" and "(student) is rejected by others") and negative peer behaviors (e.g., "(student) fights with other students" and "(student) picks on smaller or weaker students"). Controlling for pretests, the TAI students were rated significantly higher than control students on the friendship scale in Experiments 1 and 2 (Slavin, Leavey, and Madden, 1982). On the negative peer behavior scale, TAI students were rated significantly better in Experiment 1 and marginally better ($p<.10$) in Experiment 2.

The one Jigsaw study to investigate liking of classmates (Blaney, Stephan, Rosenfield, Aronson, and Sikes, 1977) found no differences on ratings of classmates, but found that control students felt that they were liked by their classmates more consistently than did Jigsaw students. Many of the Learning Together studies have used responses to such questions as "Other students like me as I am" to assess students' feelings of being liked. Positive effects on such measures have been reported by Johnson, Johnson, Johnson, and Anderson (1976), Cooper, Johnson, Johnson, and Wilderson (1980), Johnson and Johnson (1981), R. T. Johnson and D. W. Johnson (in press b), and D. W. Johnson and R. T. Johnson (in press). A few studies (Slavin and Wodarski, 1978; Madden and Slavin, in press; DeVries, Mescon, and Shackman, 1975b; DeVries and Mescon, 1975) found no effects on questionnaire scales measuring liking of classmates or feelings of being liked. However, all of these studies took place at the elementary level, where virtually all students report that they like their classmates very much, and this ceiling effect almost certainly accounts for these failures to find differences. The preponderance of the evidence, including the evidence from the race relations and mainstreaming studies (see Chapters 4 and 5), does support the conclusion that cooperative learning improves positive relationships between students.

Cooperation, Altruism, and the Ability to Take Another's Perspective

One non-cognitive outcome that would be anticipated as a consequence of a cooperative experience in schools is that students would become more cooperative or altruistic. Perhaps because this outcome is widely assumed, it has not been studied as often as many others.

One frequently used measure of a preference for altruism or cooperation as opposed to maximizing individual gain or competition is a choice board devised by Kagan and Madsen (1972), in which students allocate rewards to actual or imagined peers. The choices with which students are confronted are to give the "peer" more rewards (altruism), the same number of rewards (equality), or fewer rewards (competition) than the students receive themselves. Using measures based on this paradigm, Hertz-Lazarowitz, Sharan, and Steinberg (1980) showed that students who had experienced Group-Investigation made more altruistic choices than did control students. They also found that when students who had worked in cooperative groups were reassigned to new groups for an experimental task, they cooperated better and had higher group productivity than did groups made up from the control classes. A similar study (Sharan, Raviv, and Kussell, 1982) failed to replicate the reward-allocation findings, but found that when new groups were made up from among the experimental and control classes, there was more verbal and non-verbal cooperation and less competition on a Lego task among students who had experienced Group-Investigation than among control students. Students who had been in a STAD condition also exhibited more verbal and non-verbal cooperation and less competition than control students, but the Group-Investigation students evidenced more verbal and non-verbal cooperation than the STAD students. Finally, Hertz-Lazarowitz, Sapir, and Sharan (1981) found that students who had experienced Group-Investigation scored lower in competitiveness than did Jigsaw or control students. There were no differences between Jigsaw and control on this measure.

Johnson, Johnson, Johnson, and Anderson (1976) found that when students engaged in Learning Together activities, they made more altruistic choices on a task similar to the choice board than did students who had worked competitively or individualistically. Ryan and Wheeler (1977) found that students who had studied cooperatively made more cooperative and helpful decisions in a subsequent simulation game than did students who had studied competitively.

Another outcome related to cooperation is preference for cooperation or competition. Blaney, Stephan, Rosenfield, Aronson, and Sikes (1977) found that, following an experience with Jigsaw, students expressed less agreement with the statement "I would rather beat a classmate at school-work than help him" than did control students. Wheeler and Ryan (1973) also documented a positive effect of cooperative classroom experience on student attitudes toward cooperation.

Finally, an important component of the ability to cooperate with others is the ability to understand someone else's perspective. Bridgeman (1977) found that students who had worked cooperatively using Jigsaw were better able to take the perspective of another person than were control students, and Johnson, Johnson, Johnson, and Anderson (1976) found that students who had worked cooperatively were better able to identify feelings in taped conversations than were students who had worked individually.

Thus it is clear that cooperative experiences do increase components of cooperative and altruistic behaviors more than do competitive or individualistic experiences. These findings are very important, because they suggest that cooperative learning may produce positive changes in the kinds of pro-social behaviors that are increasingly needed in a society in which the ability to get along with others is more and more crucial. However, it is possible that these effects are due in part to a social desirability bias on the part of students who have just gone through a cooperative experience. It must be apparent to such students that if they have just gone through several weeks of cooperative work, in which the importance of cooperation and caring about groupmates has been repeatedly expressed, they are expected to give altruistic or pro-cooperative responses on a post-test. This line of research would be strengthened by follow-up assessments by independent testers long enough after the conclusion of the study to allow any social desirability bias to wear off.

Conclusion

The breadth of the outcomes affected by cooperative learning strategies is impressive. There exist special programs focused solely on improving student self-esteem, or internal locus of control, or race relations, or mainstreaming, or achievement, but cooperative learning strategies have been shown to positively influence all of these outcomes and several others. What is more remarkable is that each of several quite different methods has been shown to have positive effects on a wide variety of outcomes. The differences in patterns of non-cognitive outcomes between methods are not as interesting as their similarities. In general, for any desired outcome of schooling, administer a cooperative learning treatment, and about one-half to two-thirds of the time there will be a significant difference between the experimental and control groups in favor of the experimental groups.

Because of the generality of the findings, it could be hypothesized that the effects of cooperative learning techniques on non-cognitive outcomes are due not to any linkage between the methods and each particular outcome, but to an overall "halo" effect that produces generally positive responses to any question. However, this is unlikely, because one would think that the first variable to show an effect of a halo effect would be liking of school, the one non-cognitive variable that has been influenced least consistently by the cooperative learning methods.

It is also relatively unlikely that the effects summarized in this chapter are due to any systematic methodological bias, because the methodologies of the various studies are so different from one another. For example, "Hawthorne" effects could be a problem in some studies, but in most of the STAD, TGT, and Learning Together studies the control groups were given a special treatment with its own training procedures, as well as materials identical to those used in the experimental group, so that control teachers would also be using a "new" method. Teachers were randomly assigned to treatments or taught experimental and control classes in most studies, so at least for these studies teacher differences due to different levels of interest in a new method are not a factor. Random assignment or matching plus analysis of covariance or equivalent statistical methods insured that pre-existing differences did not account for the effects seen in any of the studies. The robustness of the findings is supported by the wide range of subject areas, student ages, geographical locations, and research methodologies and staffs used in the various studies.

While the effects of cooperative learning on the non-cognitive outcomes reviewed in this study appear to be relatively robust, there is much work yet to be done in this area. The research conducted to date has dealt primarily with validation of the various cooperative learning models of the "Brand X vs. Brand Y" variety, where Brand X is some form of cooperative learning and Brand Y is a competitive, individualistic, or untreated control treatment. There have been some factorial treatments in the TGT-STAD tradition (e.g., Hulten and DeVries, 1976; Slavin, 1978c, 1980a), but these have focused primarily on achievement outcomes. There is a need both for careful analysis of what goes on in a cooperative classroom, and for more attention to just how the various outcomes come about. A great deal is changed when a teacher adopts cooperative learning; the classroom incentive and task structures, feedback systems, authority systems, and the teacher's role all change substantially. Which of these changes accounts for the effects of cooperative learning and non-cognitive outcomes? We have enough research to begin to identify which components of cooperative learning methods impact on student achievement (see Chapter 3), but we have little to go on with respect to each of the non-cognitive outcomes discussed in this chapter.

In summary, cooperative learning has been shown in a large number and wide variety of studies to positively influence a host of important non-cognitive variables. This chapter concludes that, while there are non-systematic failures to find differences in some studies for each variable, the overall effects of cooperative learning on student self-esteem, peer support for achievement, internal locus of control, time on-task, liking of class and of classmates, cooperativeness, and other variables are positive and robust.

7

Conclusions and New Directions

Cooperative learning represents an unusual event in the history of educational research. The cooperative learning methods were based on well-established social psychological theory, constructed to meet the practical exigencies of the classroom, evaluated in several dozen methodologically adequate field experiments, and ultimately disseminated widely. At present, it is estimated that approximately twenty thousand teachers, located in every state and many foreign countries, are using Student Team Learning, and many more use the other cooperative learning methods (see Hollifield & Slavin, in press; Slavin, 1981c).

The range of positive outcomes seen in the research on cooperative learning is wide. Because cooperative learning interventions are explicitly both motivationally directed and socially directed, both motivational and social outcomes have been studied. Interestingly, regardless of the particular measure involved, about two-thirds of the cooperative learning studies that investigate any positive outcome find a significantly positive effect on it. This proportion is somewhat higher for race relations and somewhat lower for liking-of-class outcomes, but the two-to-one ratio of studies that find significantly positive effects to those that find no differences (negative effects are very rare) holds for most of the principal measures, including student achievement. Given the uncertainties of field research and the far more equivocal outcomes of many other instructional innovations, this is a remarkable record.

The major conclusions of the research presented in Chapters 3–6 are summarized below.

Academic Achievement. Overall, the effects of cooperative learning on student achievement are positive. Of forty-one studies that met minimum methodological adequacy and duration criteria, twenty-six (63%) found higher achievement in cooperative learning than in control conditions, fourteen (34%) found no differences, and one (2%) found greater achievement for a control group. The most consistent effects were the main effects; race X treatment interactions showing especially great gains for black students in the cooperative groups were the only interactions that were consistent in direction, although the possibility of complex ability X treatment interactions cannot be discarded.

Examinations of the relative achievement outcomes of the different methods and component analyses of some of the methods indicate convincingly that the effects of cooperative learning on student achievement come about because cooperative incentives motivate students to encourage each other to learn, not because group study is in itself an effective strategy. The most effective cooperative incentive structures are ones in which group rewards depend on the sum of the learning performances of group members, and in which each student is individually accountable to the group for his or her learning. Excluding studies in which task specialization is used, methods that involve specific group rewards based on their members' individual learning had positive effects on student achievement in twenty-two (88%) of twenty-five studies, while none of the nine studies that used neither groups rewards based on individual group members' learning nor task specialization found positive achievement effects. Three component analyses also found that while group rewards based on group members' learning contributed to student achievement, group study by itself did not. Other features that may contribute to the effectiveness of certain cooperative learning methods for achievement include equal opportunity scoring procedures (i.e., rewards for improvement) and, for some areas of social studies, task specialization (where each student has a unique task within the group). Use of group competition appears to add to the achievement effects only in so far as it is one way of providing group rewards based on group members' learning.

Intergroup Relations. The research on the effects of cooperative learning on friendships between black, white, Mexican-American, and other students (as measured by sociometric instruments and behavioral observations) clearly shows that cooperative learning increases cross-ethnic friendship choices. Eleven of fourteen studies on this topic have found some benefit of cooperative learning for intergroup relations, although not every study found positive effects on every measure of intergroup relations. Two studies found long-term maintenance of increased cross-ethnic friendship choices, and a secondary analysis of one of these studies found that the treatment effects were strongest for close, reciprocated friendship choices. At present, it is unclear whether these effects are simply consequences of more frequent contact across ethnic group lines or whether the cooperative incentive structure has a direct positive effect on development of positive relations.

Mainstreaming and Special Education. A recent and growing focus of cooperative learning research is on relationships between academically handicapped students (e.g., learning disabled, educable mentally retarded) and their non-handicapped classmates in mainstreamed classrooms. The cooperative learning research on this topic indicates that use of cooperative learning methods does generally result in greater acceptance of academically handicapped students (i.e., more friendship and interaction and less rejection). Seven of ten studies involving mainstreamed classrooms found some positive effects on acceptance of or interaction with academically or emotionally handicapped students, although the effects have been less consistent than those for intergroup relations. In the two studies in which achievement was measured, gains in achievement for the entire class were found along with the gains in cross-handicap acceptance. Two studies in self-contained classrooms for emotionally disturbed adolescents indicated positive effects of TGT on student behavior, but not achievement.

Other Non-Cognitive Outcomes. In addition to the intergroup relations and mainstreaming outcomes discussed above, cooperative learning methods have had positive effects on a number of important non-cognitive outcomes. Perhaps the most important is self-esteem; most of the major cooperative learning methods (STAD, TGT, TAI, Jigsaw, and Learning Together) have found positive effects on some aspect of self-esteem in at least one study. Several of the non-cognitive outcomes are related to achievement effects. Many of the STAD and TGT studies found that cooperative learning students felt their classmates wanted them to do well more often than did control students. These peer norms favoring achievement play a central role in the theory linking cooperative learning to achievement outlined in Chapter 3. A few studies also found that students who experienced cooperative learning were more likely than control students to feel that their success or failure in school depended on their own efforts, rather than on luck or external factors. Students who hold these beliefs (internal locus of control) have been found in many studies to have higher achievement and motivation than students who believe that luck or external factors determine their success (external locus of control). Finally, time on-task is an important precondition for learning; most of the major cooperative learning methods, especially the Student Team Learning studies, have been found to have positive effects on time on-task or on teacher ratings of students' behavior in class.

Surprisingly, the non-cognitive measure on which an observer of any cooperative learning classroom would most confidently predict effects is the measure on which effects have been most inconsistent. Only half of the studies measuring students' liking of class have found greater liking of class in cooperative learning than in control groups. Ceiling effects may explain part of this failure to find significant differences, but this is still an unexpected result. On the other hand, students' liking of their classmates and feelings of being liked by them have been more consistently increased by cooperative learning. Finally, most studies that assessed the effects of cooperative learning on the ability or predisposition to cooperate found such effects.

Next Steps

As noted earlier, this book should be seen as an interim report on cooperative learning research. As of this writing, research on cooperative learning is being expanded in many directions. New cooperative learning methods are being developed and evaluated, applications of cooperative learning to such problems as delinquency prevention, drug-abuse prevention, and improved relationships across sex lines are being studied, different cooperative learning methods are being compared, and important advances in the theory of cooperative learning are being made by means of component analyses and more sophisticated measures. A book on cooperative learning written five years from now will hopefully be far more sophisticated in terms of an understanding of the potential, the limitations, and the theory of cooperative learning.

In order to arrive at this happy state, a great deal of work must be done. The sections below touch on a few of the many unresolved issues that should be researched over the next few years.

Unresolved Issues: Achievement

Perhaps the most important question about the effects of cooperative learning on student achievement is why they occur. Chapter 3 presents evidence to indicate that the effective component of cooperative learning is specific group rewards based on group members' individual learning. However, the mechanisms by which group rewards increase student achievement are only dimly understood. Detailed observational studies or interview studies might illuminate these mechanisms. We really do not know what specific behaviors and perceptions are activated by group rewards. Do group rewards increase student achievement by motivating students to work harder themselves, or by motivating them to help their groupmates? Important questions relating to this issue might include the importance of the size or nature of group rewards; for example, does it make any difference whether group grades, tangible rewards, or simply recognition are used? Does it matter whether group competition is used as the standard for group success, or would other standards be more or less effective? What are the effects of group success and group failure on student achievement and achievement related perceptions?

The effects of task specialization are poorly understood at present. Cooperative learning methods that use task specialization (e.g., Jigsaw and Group-Investigation) also have many other features. An experiment directly comparing group study and task specialization is needed.

Unfortunately, only one study (the Ziegler [1981] Jigsaw II study) has assessed long-term retention as an outcome of cooperative learning. Also, only a small number of studies have assessed use of cooperative learning methods over a full school year or over several subjects in a school day. More research along these lines is needed to establish whether the most appropriate use of cooperative learning methods is as a supplement to traditional methods or as a primary means of providing instruction.

Equal-opportunity scoring methods, such as those used in STAD, TGT, and TAI, are interesting interventions in their own right, and warrant further study as components of cooperative learning methods. The effects of these methods on student attributions, perceived probability of success, and other perceptions would be particularly important to assess.

The issue of possible ability by treatment interactions is an important one. Cooperative learning may be differentially effective for different students. Ability by treatment interactions are not uncommon in cooperative learning studies, but they are inconsistent in direction and form. Further research is needed to discover if there are such interactions, when they are likely to be seen, and why they occur (if they do). Similarly, the race by treatment interactions seen in a few studies need to be replicated and, if they in fact exist, explained.

Cooperative learning methods may also be more effective in some subjects than others, or more effective at some grade levels than others (although the evidence to date does not support such interactions). It is possible that certain cooperative learning methods are best used to teach basic skills while others are best for concepts, but there is almost no evidence on this at present.

Finally, there is always a need for evaluations of new forms of cooperative learning. New methods are needed to take on such subjects as writing, reading, laboratory science, and foreign language (including English as a second language). Alternative ways of using cooperative learning in the subjects in which it has most often been used (e.g., mathematics, language arts, social studies) are also needed. The analysis presented in Chapter 3 would have been impossible if many researchers had not evaluated a wide range of cooperative learning methods, although at this point, systematic variations in methods are more needed than more completely new techniques.

Unresolved Issues: Intergroup Relations and Acceptance of Mainstreamed Students

The theoretical models behind the effects of cooperative learning on interethnic relations and effects on acceptance of mainstreamed students are probably quite similar, but while there is enough evidence to indicate that the effects are positive, the mechanisms by which cooperative learning affects student relationships are unclear. Several types of research are needed in these areas.

First, it is important to establish the extent to which cooperative learning really changes cross-ethnic and cross-handicap relations. Out-of-class and out-of-school observations to indicate persistence of such relationships outside of the classroom setting are especially needed. This issue could also be approached by interviewing students concerning their out-of-class interactions with their classmates, to see how much carryover there is from heterogeneous friendships formed in cooperative learning interventions. Carryover of cross-ethnic and cross-handicap friendships to generalized attitudes toward other ethnicities or handicaps also need to be assessed in more detail.

A very important theoretical issue to be resolved is how cooperative learning methods affect relationships between students who have never been assigned to the same group. Is there a spinoff in which students become friends of their groupmates' friends, or would students have to be on many teams to develop positive relationships with all of their classmates? Use or non-use of group competition may affect this process, and should also be investigated. Finally, it may be that valuable group rewards (such as grades or tangibles) would act to increase within-group cohesion at the expense of out-group friendships, while smaller rewards (such as recognition or free time) would have different effects. Group success or failure may have important effects on within- and across-team friendships, and their effects may depend on the level and character of group rewards used.

Another important theoretical issue raised in Chapter 4 is whether cooperative goals are needed to improve intergroup or cross-handicap relations, or whether contact is the only important variable. If cooperative goals do make a contribution, do they operate through increased contact, or do they have a direct effect on positive relationships? Detailed observational or interview studies might be one way to get at these mechanisms, although continued component analyses are also important. Also, the importance of equal achievement or perceptions of equal ability for formation of heterogeneous friendships needs to be studied further, including studies of equal-opportunity scoring methods on such perceptions.

Finally, it is important to understand whether or not the effects of cooperative learning operate in different ways for friendships from and toward black, Mexican-American, and Anglo students, or toward students with varying kinds and degrees of handicaps. It may be that the model linking cooperative learning to improvements in cross-ethnic relations is quite different from that explaining effects on cross-handicap relations.

Other Unresolved Issues

- How real and how lasting are the effects of cooperative learning on student self-esteem? What features of cooperative learning contribute to these effects? Could they be due to increased opportunities for success rather than to the group experience?
- How real and how lasting are the effects of cooperative learning on student internal locus of control? Are these effects simply

results of students' feeling more successful, or do students truly perceive a closer link between their actions and their outcomes?

- How important are increases in time on-task in explaining improvements in student achievement brought about by cooperative learning?
- What are the effects of cooperative learning on student attendance?
- Would better measures of liking of school or liking of class show more consistently positive results for cooperative learning, or does the inconsistency of these findings have substantive meaning?
- What are the consequences (in terms of such variables are self-esteem, motivation, peer support for academic achievement, or ultimate mental health) of the improvements in general liking of classmates brought about by cooperative learning?
- Do cooperative learning methods have long-term effects on students' predispositions to cooperate or to be altruistic in situations in which cooperation or competition are alternative responses? Would too much of an emphasis on cooperation impair students' ability to compete?
- What are the effects of cooperative learning experiences over a longer period on student mental health?
- Are there simpler cooperative learning methods that would be as effective as the existing techniques for the various academic and social outcomes?
- Would training in group interaction skills, peer tutoring methods, or other skills improve the achievement outcomes of cooperative learning methods? Would they improve intergroup relations or attitudes toward academically handicapped students?
- What effect might cooperative learning have on preventing delinquency or resocializing delinquent adolescents?
- Can a way be found to capture the power of peer norms favoring achievement without using small face-to-face groups? For example, could whole classes be defined as "teams" and rewarded for improvement?
- Can cooperative learning methods be extended to students' entire instructional program? Can cooperative learning be used indefinitely?
- What kinds of institutional supports and training methods are most likely to lead to effective use by teachers of cooperative learning methods?
- Could variations of cooperative learning be used in bilingual education, where (for example) Spanish-speaking students could learn English in cooperation with English-speaking students learning Spanish?

- Can cooperative learning methods (or modifications) be used effectively in self-contained classes for learning disabled students?
- Can cooperative learning methods (or modifications) be used effectively in programs for the gifted?

As the long list above indicates, there are many important theoretical as well as practical issues yet to be resolved in research on cooperative learning. However, the research done up to the present has shown enough positive effects of cooperative learning on a variety of outcomes to force us to re-examine traditional instructional practices. We can no longer ignore the potential power of the peer group, perhaps the one remaining free resource for improving schools. We can no longer see the class as thirty or more individuals whose only instructionally useful interactions are with the teacher, where peer interactions are unstructured or off-task. On the other hand, at least for achievement, we now know that simply allowing students to work together is unlikely to capture the power of the peer group to motivate students to perform; structured methods with group rewards based on group members' demonstrated learning appear to be needed. For intergroup relations, acceptance of mainstreamed students, and general attraction among students, it is not yet clear whether structured groups and group rewards are absolutely necessary, but it is clear that these outcomes can be reliably produced at the same time as achievement and other outcomes are being improved for the entire class. This is a revolutionary development for attempts to improve intergroup and cross-handicap relationships, as programs designed only to improve relationships are seen as "frills" by many school districts, and are not supported if they take time away from instruction.

As cooperative learning methods become more sophisticated and more widely used, we will need to reopen a fundamental issue of educational philosophy: How do we want to socialize our children? Even if instructional methods are developed that are as effective or more effective than cooperative learning for increasing student achievement, we will have to consider what the longterm effects of cooperative learning (or any alternative) might be. If adolescents and adults had had school experiences that were social instead of isolated, successful instead of frustrating, enhancing of self-esteem instead of deleterious to it, we might see improvements in their mental health. If the typical school experience was one based on cooperative principles, could we still have the alienation, boredom and inevitable failure that so many adolescents experience? Even forgetting the particular outcomes measured in the research on cooperative learning methods, it simply seems logical that a humane, engaging, and social instructional system should create a better environment in which to raise children to responsible adult roles and self-acceptance as adults. The real importance of the research discussed in this book is that it forces us to choose between two equally practical alternatives: continuing along the lines of traditional instructional methods, or building a fundamentally new instructional system based on cooperative learning principles. We cannot afford not to choose.

References

Allen, W., and VanSickle, R. Instructional effects of learning teams for low achieving students. Unpublished manuscript, University of Georgia, 1981.

Allport, G. *The Nature of Prejudice.* Cambridge, MA: Addison-Wesley, 1954.

Ames, C., Ames, R., and Felker, D. W. Effects of competitive reward structure and valence of outcome on children's achievement attributions. *Journal of Educational Psychology,* 1977, *69,* 1–8.

Amir, Y. Contact hypothesis of ethnic relations. *Psychological Bulletin,* 1969, *71,* 319–343.

Anderson, L. M. Student response to seatwork: Implications for the study of students' cognitive processing. Paper presented at the annual convention of the American Educational Research Association, Los Angeles, 1981.

Armstrong, B., Johnson, D. W., and Balow, B. Effects of cooperative vs. individualistic learning experiences on interpersonal attraction between learning-disabled and normal-progress elementary school students. *Contemporary Educational Psychology,* 1981, *6,* 102–109.

Aronson, E. *The Jigsaw Classroom.* Beverly Hills, CA: Sage, 1978.

Atkinson, J. W. Towards experimental analysis of human motivation in terms of motives, expectancies, and incentives. In J. W. Atkinson (ed.), *Motives in Fantasy, Action, and Society.* Princeton, NJ: Van Nostrand, 1958.

Ballard, M., Corman, L., Gottlieb, J., and Kaufman, M. Improving the social status of mainstreamed retarded children. *Journal of Educational Psychology,* 1977, *69,* 605–611.

Baltimore City Schools. A report of the study group on school attendance/dropouts. Baltimore, Maryland, 1972.

Beady, C., and Slavin, R. E. Making success available to all students in desegregated schools. *Integrated Education,* 1981, *18(6),* 28–31.

Beady, C. L., Slavin, R. E., and Fennessey, G. M. Alternative student evaluation structures and a focused schedule of instruction in an inner-city junior high school. *Journal of Educational Psychology,* 1981, *73,* 518–523.

Beaman, A., Diener, E., Fraser, S., and Endressen, K. Effects of voluntary and semi-voluntary peer-monitoring programs on academic performance. *Journal of Educational Psychology,* 1977, *69,* 109–114.

Bjorkland, R., Johnson, R., and Krotee, M. Effects of cooperative, competitive, and individualistic goal structures on golf skills. Unpublished manuscript, University of Minnesota, 1980.

Blaney, N. T., Stephan, S., Rosenfield, D., Aronson, E., and Sikes, J. Interdependence in the classroom: A field study. *Journal of Educational Psychology*, 1977, *69(2)*, 121–128.

Bossert, S. Tasks, group management, and teacher control behavior: A study of classroom organization and teacher style. *School Review*, 1977, *85*, 552–565.

Brewer, M. In-group bias in the minimal intergroup situation: A cognitive-motivational analysis. *Psychological Bulletin*, 1979, *86*, 307–324.

Bridgeman, D. The influence of cooperative, interdependent learning on role taking and moral reasoning: A theoretical and empirical field study with fifth grade students. Unpublished doctoral dissertation, University of California, Santa Cruz, 1977.

Brookover, W., Beady, C., Flood, P., Schweitzer, J., and Wisenbaker, J. *School Social Systems and Student Achievement*. New York: Praeger, 1979.

Brophy, J. E. Teacher behavior and its effects. *Journal of Educational Psychology*, 1979, *71*, 733–750.

Bruininks, V. L. Peer status and personality characteristics of learning disabled and non-disabled students. *Journal of Learning Disabilities*, 1978, *11*, 29–34.

Bruininks, V. L., Rynders, J. E., and Gross, J. C. Social acceptance of mildly retarded pupils in resource rooms and regular classes. *American Journal of Mental Deficiency*, 1974, *78*, 377–383.

Bruning, J., Sommer, D., and Jones, B. The motivational effects of cooperation and competition in the means-independent situation. *Journal of Social Psychology*, 1966, *68*, 269–274.

Bryan, T. Peer popularity of learning disabled children. *Journal of Learning Disabilities*, 1974, *7*, 621–625.

Bryan, T. Peer popularity of learning disabled students: A replication. *Journal of Learning Disabilities*, 1976, *9*, 307–311.

Burnstein, E., and Worchel, P. Arbitrariness of frustration and its consequences for aggression in a social situation. *Journal of Personality*, 1962, *30*, 528–540.

Busching, B. C., and Busching, B. A. Standards of evaluation and cooperative versus competitive rewarding of high and low achievers. *Journal of Experimental Education*, in press.

Campbell, D., and Stanley, J. *Experimental and Quasi-Experimental Designs for Research*. Chicago: Rand McNally, 1963.

Chennault, M. Improving the social acceptance of unpopular educable retarded pupils in special classes. *American Journal of Mental Deficiency*, 1967, *72*, 455–458.

Clifford, M. M. A revised measure of locus of control. *Child Study Journal*, 1976, *6*, 85–90.

Cohen, E. G. The effects of desegregation on race relations. *Law and Contemporary Problems*, 1975, *39*, 271–299.

Cohen, E. G., and Roper, S. Modification of interracial interaction disability: An application of status characteristic theory. *American Sociological Review*, 1972, *37*, 643–657.

Cohen, J., and Cohen, P. *Applied Multiple Regression/Correlation Analysis for the Behavioral Sciences*. Hillsdale, NJ: Lawrence Erlbaum Associates, 1975.

Coleman, J. S. *The Adolescent Society*. New York: The Free Press of Glencoe, 1961.

Coleman, J. S., Campbell, E., Hobson, C., McPartland, J., Mood, A., Weinfeld,

F., and York, R. Equality of educational opportunity. U.S. Department of Health, Education, and Welfare, 1966.

Cook, S. W. Motives in a conceptual analysis of attitude-related behavior. In W. Arnold and D. Levine (eds.), *Nebraska Symposium on Motivation* (vol. 17). Lincoln: University of Nebraska Press, 1969.

Cook, S. W. Interpersonal and attitudinal outcomes of cooperating interracial groups. *Journal of Research and Development in Education*, 1978, *12*, 97–113.

Cook, S. W. Social science and school desegregation: Did we mislead the Supreme Court? *Personality and Social Psychology Bulletin*, 1979, *5*, 420–437.

Cooper, L., Johnson, D. W., Johnson, R., and Wilderson, F. Effects of cooperative, competitive, and individualistic experiences on interpersonal attraction among heterogeneous peers. *Journal of Social Psychology*, 1980, *111*, 243–252.

Coopersmith, S. A. *The Antecedents of Self-Esteem*. San Francisco: Freeman, 1967.

Crain, R., and Mahard, R. Desegregation and black achievement: A review of the research. *Law and Contemporary Problems*, 1978, *42*, 17–56.

Crombag, H. F. Cooperation and competition in means-interdependent triads. *Journal of Personality and Social Psychology*, 1966, *4*, 692–695.

DeCharms, R. Affiliation motivation and productivity in small groups. *Journal of Abnormal and Social Psychology*, 1957, *55*, 222–226.

Deutsch, M. An experimental study of the effects of cooperation and competition upon group process. *Human Relations*, 1949, *2*, 199–231. (a)

Deutsch, M. A theory of cooperation and competition. *Human Relations*, 1949, *2*, 129–152. (b)

Deutsch, M. Education and distributive justice: Some reflections on grading systems. *American Psychologist*, 1979, *34*, 391–401.

Devin-Sheehan, L., Feldman, R. S., and Allen, V. L. Research on children tutoring children: A critical review. *Review of Educational Research*, 1976, *46(3)*, 355–385.

DeVoe, M. V. Cooperation as a function of self-concept, sex, and race. *Educational Research Quarterly*, 1977, *2(2)*, 1–8.

DeVries, D. L., and Edwards, K. J. Learning games and student teams: Their effects on classroom process. *American Educational Research Journal*, 1973, *10*, 307–318.

DeVries, D. L., and Edwards, K. J. Student teams and learning games: Their effects on cross-race and cross-sex interaction. *Journal of Educational Psychology*, 1974, *66*, 741–749.

DeVries, D. L., Edwards, K J., and Slavin, R. E. Biracial learning teams and race relations in the classroom: Four field experiments on Teams-Games-Tournament. *Journal of Educational Psychology*, 1978, *70*, 356–362.

DeVries, D. L., Edwards, K. J., and Wells, E. H. Teams-Games-Tournament in the social studies classroom: Effects on academic achievement, student attitudes, cognitive beliefs, and classroom climate. Center for Social Organization of Schools, The Johns Hopkins University, 1974. Report No. 173. (a)

DeVries, D. L., Edwards, K. J., and Wells, E. H. Team competition effects on classroom group process. Center for Social Organization of Schools, The Johns Hopkins University, 1974. Report No. 174. (b)

DeVries, D., Lucasse, P., and Shackman, S. Small group versus individualized instruction: A field test of their relative effectiveness. Paper presented at the annual convention of the American Psychological Association, New York, 1979.

DeVries, D. L., and Mescon, I. T. Teams-Games-Tournament: An effective task and reward structure in the elementary grades. Center for Social Organization of Schools, The Johns Hopkins University, 1975. Report No. 189.

DeVries, D. L., Mescon, I. T., and Shackman, S. L. Teams-Games-Tournament (TGT) effects on reading skills in the elementary grades. Center for Social Organization of Schools, The Johns Hopkins University, 1975. Report No. 200. (a)

DeVries, D. L., Mescon, I. T., and Shackman, S. L. Teams-Games-Tournament in the elementary classroom: A replication. Center for Social Organization of Schools, The Johns Hopkins University, 1975. Report No. 190. (b)

DeVries, D. L., and Slavin, R. E. Teams-Games-Tournament (TGT): Review of ten classroom experiments. *Journal of Research and Development in Education*, 1978, *12*, 28–38.

DeVries, D. L., Slavin, R. E., Fennessey, G. M., Edwards, K. J., and Lombardo, M. M. *Teams-Games-Tournament: The Team Learning Approach*. Englewood Cliffs, NJ: Educational Technology Publications, 1980.

DuCette, J. Locus of control and academic achievement. Paper presented at the annual convention of the American Psychological Association, New York, 1979.

Dunn, L. M. Special education for the mildly retarded: Is much of it justified? *Exceptional Children*, 1968, *35*, 5–22.

Dunn, R. E., and Goldman, M. Competition and non-competition in relationship to satisfaction and feelings toward own-group and non-group members. *Journal of Social Psychology*, 1966, *68*, 299–311.

Edwards, K. J., and DeVries, D. L. Learning games and student teams: Their effects on student attitudes and achievement. Center for Social Organization of Schools, The Johns Hopkins University, 1972. Report No. 147.

Edwards, K. J., and DeVries, D. L. The effects of Teams-Games-Tournament and two structural variations on classroom process, student attitudes, and student achievement. Center for Social Organization of Schools, The Johns Hopkins University, 1974. Report No. 172.

Edwards, K. J., DeVries, D. L., and Snyder, J. P. Games and teams: A winning combination. *Simulation and Games*, 1972, *3*, 247–269.

Faust, W. Group vs. individual problem-solving. *Journal of Abnormal and Social Psychology*, 1959, *59*, 68–72.

Fraser, S., Beaman, A., Diener, E., and Kelem, R. Two, three, or four heads are better than one: Modification of college performance by peer monitoring. *Journal of Educational Psychology*, 1977, *69*, 101–108.

Garibaldi, A. The affective contributions of cooperative and group goal structures. *Journal of Educational Psychology*, 1979, *71*, 788–795.

Geffner, R. The effects of interdependent learning on self-esteem, interethnic relations, and intra-ethnic attitudes of elementary school children: A field experiment. Unpublished doctoral dissertation, University of California, Santa Cruz, 1978.

Gerard, H. B., and Hoyt, M. F. Distinctiveness of social categorization and attitude toward ingroup members. *Journal of Personality and Social Psychology*, 1974, *29*, 836–842.

Gerard, H. B., and Miller, N. *School Desegregation: A Long-Range Study*. New York, NY: Plenum Press, 1975.

Gnagney, W. The comparative effects of small groups vs. teacher-led discussion sessions upon student achievement and perception in educational psychology. *Journal of Educational Research*, 1962, *56*, 28.

Gonzales, A. Classroom cooperation and ethnic balance. Paper presented at the annual convention of the American Psychological Association, New York, 1979.

Gonzales, A. An approach to interdependent/cooperative bilingual education and measures related to social motives. Unpublished manuscript, California State University at Fresno, 1981.

Good, T., and Grouws, D. The Missouri Mathematics Effectiveness Project: An experimental study in fourth grade classrooms. *Journal of Educational Psychology*, 1979, *71*, 355–362.

Goodman, H., Gottlieb, J., and Harrison, R. H. Social acceptance of EMRs integrated into a non-graded elementary school. *American Jounal of Mental Deficiency*, 1972, *76*, 412–417.

Gordon, K. Group judgements in the field of lifted weights. *Journal of Experimental Psychology*, 1924, *7*, 398–400.

Gottlieb, J., Semmel, M. I., and Veldman, D. J. Correlates of social status among mainstreamed mentally retarded children. *Journal of Educational Psychology*, 1978, *70*, 396–405.

Granovetter, M. The strength of weak ties. *American Journal of Sociology*, 1973, *78*, 1360–1380.

Graziano, W., French, D., Brownell, C., and Hartup, W. Peer interaction in same- and mixed-age triads in relation to chronological age and incentive condition. *Child Development*, 1976, *47*, 707–714.

Grossack, M. M. Some effects of cooperation and competition upon small group behavior. *Journal of Abnormal and Social Psychology*, 1954, *49*, 341–348.

Gurnee, H. Learning under competitive and collaborative sets. *Journal of Experimental Social Psychology*, 1968, *4*, 26–34.

Haines, D. B., and McKeachie, W. J. Cooperation versus competitive discussion methods in teaching introductory psychology. *Journal of Educational Psychology*, 1967, *58*, 386–390.

Hallinan, M. Children's friendships and cliques. *Social Psychology Quarterly*, 1979, *42*, 43–54.

Hamblin, R. L., Hathaway, C., and Wodarski, J. S. Group contingencies, peer tutoring, and accelerating academic achievement. In E. Ramp and W. Hopkins (eds.), *A New Direction for Education: Behavior Analysis*. Lawrence, Kansas: The University of Kansas, Department of Human Development, 1971, 41–53.

Hammond, L. K., and Goldman, M. Competition and non-competition and its relationship to individual and group productivity. *Sociometry*, 1961, *24*, 46–60.

Hansell, S., and Slavin, R. E. Cooperative learning and the structure of interracial friendships. *Sociology of Education*, 1981, *54*, 98–106.

Hansell, S., Tackaberry, S. N., and Slavin, R. E. Cooperation, competition, and the structure of student peer groups. *Social Psychology Quarterly*, in press.

Hare, B. R. Racial and sociometric variations in preadolescent area-specific and general self-esteem. *International Journal of Intercultural Relations*, 1977, *1*, 31–51.

Hersen, M., and Barlow, D. *Single Case Experimental Designs*. New York: Pergamon Press, 1976.

Hertz-Lazarowitz, R., Sharan, S., and Sapir, C. Academic and social effects of two cooperative learning methods in desegregated classrooms. Paper presented at the annual convention of the American Educational Research Association, New York, 1982.

Hertz-Lazarowitz, R., Sharan, S., and Steinberg, R. Classroom learning styles and cooperative behavior of elementary school children. *Journal of Educational Psychology*, 1980, *72*, 99–106.

Hollifield, J., and Slavin, R. E. Disseminating Student Team Learning through federally funded programs: Appropriate technology, appropriate channels. *Knowledge*, in press.

Huber, G., Bogatzki, W., and Winter, M. Cooperation: Condition and goal of teaching and learning in classrooms. Unpublished manuscript, University of Tubingen, Germany, 1982.

Hudgins, B. Effects of group experience on individual problem solving. *Journal of Educational Psychology*, 1960, *51*, 37–42.

Hulten, B. H., and DeVries, D. L. Team competition and group practice: Effects on student achievement and attitudes. Center for Social Organization of Schools, The Johns Hopkins University, 1976. Report No. 212.

Humphreys, B., Johnson, R., and Johnson, D. W. Effects of cooperative, competitive, and individualistic learning on students' achievement in science class. *Journal of Research in Science Teaching*, 1982, *19*, 351–356.

Hurlock, E. B. Use of group rivalry as an incentive. *Journal of Abnormal and Social Psychology*, 1927, *22*, 278–290.

Iano, R. P., Ayers, D., Heller, H. B., McGettigan, T. F., and Walker, V. S. Sociometric status of retarded children in an integrative program. *Exceptional Children*, 1974, *41*, 267–271.

Janke, R. The Teams-Games-Tournament (TGT) method and the behavioral adjustment and academic achievement of emotionally impaired adolescents. Paper presented at the annual convention of the American Educational Research Association, Toronto, 1978.

Johnson, D. W. Letter to the editor in response to Slavin's "A policy choice: Cooperative or competitive learning." *Character*, 1981, *2(5)*, 8–9.

Johnson, D. W., and Johnson, R. T. Instructional goal structure: Cooperative, competitive, or individualistic. *Review of Educational Research*, 1974, *44*, 213–240.

Johnson, D. W., and Johnson, R. T. *Learning together and alone*. Englewood Cliffs, NJ: Prentice-Hall, 1975.

Johnson, D. W., and Johnson, R. T. Conflict in the classroom: Controversy and learning. *Review of Educational Research*, 1979, *49*, 51–70.

Johnson, D. W., and Johnson, R. T. Effects of cooperative and individualistic learning experiences on interethnic interaction. *Journal of Educational Psychology*, 1981, *73*, 444–449.

Johnson, D. W., and Johnson, R. T. The integration of the handicapped into the regular classroom: Effects of cooperative and individualistic instruction. *Contemporary Educational Psychology*, in press.

Johnson, D. W., Johnson, R. T., Johnson, J., and Anderson, D. The effects of cooperative vs. individualized instruction on student prosocial behavior, attitudes toward learning, and achievement. *Journal of Educational Psychology*, 1976, *68*, 446–452.

Johnson, D. W., Johnson, R. T., and Scott, L. The effects of cooperative and individualized instruction on student attitudes and achievement. *Journal of Social Psychology*, 1978, *104*, 207–216.

Johnson, D. W., Johnson. R. T., and Skon, L. Student achievement on different types of tasks under cooperative, competitive, and individualistic conditions. *Contemporary Educational Psychology*, 1979, *4*, 99–106.

Johnson, D. W., and Johnson, S. The effects of attitude similarity, expectation of goal facilitation, and actual goal facilitation on interpersonal attraction. *Journal of Experimental Social Psychology*, 1972, *8*, 197–206.

Johnson, D. W., Maruyama, G., Johnson, R. T., Nelson, D., and Skon, L. Effects of cooperative, competitive, and individualistic goal structures on achievement: A meta-analysis. *Psychological Bulletin*, 1981, *89*, 47–62.

Johnson, G. O. A study of the social position of the mentally retarded child in the regular grades. *American Journal of Mental Deficiency*, 1950, *55*, 60–89.

Johnson, R. T., and Johnson, D. W. Type of task and student achievement and attitudes in interpersonal cooperation, competition, and individualization. *Journal of Social Psychology*, 1979, *108*, 37–48.

Johnson, R. T., and Johnson, D. W. Building friendships between handicapped and nonhandicapped students: Effects of cooperative and individualistic instruction. *American Educational Research Journal*, in press. (a)

Johnson, R. T., and Johnson, D. W. Effects of cooperative and competitive learning experiences on interpersonal attraction between handicapped and nonhandicapped students. *Journal of Social Psychology*, in press. (b)

Johnson, R. T., and Johnson, D. W. Effects of cooperative, competitive, and individualistic learning experiences on cross-handicap relationships and social development. *Exceptional Children*, in press. (c)

Johnson, R. T., Johnson, D. W., and Rynders, J. Effects of cooperative, competitive, and individualistic experiences on self-esteem of handicapped and nonhandicapped students. *Journal of Psychology*, 1981, *108*, 31–34.

Johnson, R. T., Rynders, J., Johnson, D. W., Schmidt, B., and Haider, S. Interaction between handicapped and nonhandicapped teenagers as a function of situational goal structuring: Implications for mainstreaming. *American Educational Research Journal*, 1979, *16*, 161–167.

Jones, S. C., and Vroom, V. H. Division of labor and performance under cooperative and competitive conditions. *Journal of Abnormal and Social Psychology*, 1964, *68(3)*, 313–320.

Julian, J. W., and Perry, F. A. Cooperation contrasted with intra-group and inter-group competition. *Sociometry*, 1967, *30*, 79–90.

Kagan, S., and Madsen, M. C. Cooperation and competition of Mexican, Mexican-American, and Anglo-American children of two ages under four instructional sets. *Developmental Psychology*, 1971, *5*, 32–39.

Kagan, S., and Madsen, M. C. Rivalry in Anglo-American and Mexican-American Children. *Journal of Personality and Social Psychology*, 1972, *24*, 214–220.

Klugman, S. F. Cooperative versus individual efficiency in problem solving. *Journal of Educational Psychology*, 1944, *34*, 91–100.

Kukla, A. Foundations of an attributional theory of performance. *Psychological Review*, 1972, *79*, 454–470.

Lapp, E. A. A study of the social development of slow-learning children who were assigned part-time to regular classes. *American Journal of Mental Deficiency*, 1957, *62*, 254–262.

Laughlin, P., and Bitz, D. Individual versus dyadic performance on a dysjunctive task as a function of initial ability level. *Journal of Personality and Social Psychology*, 1975, *31*, 487–496.

Laughlin, P., Branch, L., and Johnson, H. Individual versus triadic performance on a unidimensional complementary task as a function of initial ability level. *Journal of Personality and Social Psychology*, 1969, *12*, 144–150.

Laughlin, P., and Johnson, H. Group and individual performance on a complementary task as a function of initial ability level. *Journal of Experimental Social Psychology* 1966, *2*, 407–414.

Laughlin, P. R., McGlynn, R., Anderson, J., and Jacobson, E. Concept attainment by individuals versus cooperative pairs as a function of memory, sex, and concept rule. *Journal of Personality and Social Psychology*, 1968, *8*, 410–417.

Lazarowitz, R., Baird, H., Bowlden, V., and Hertz-Lazarowitz, R. Academic achievements, learning environment, and self esteem of high school students in biology taught in cooperative-investigative small groups. Unpublished manuscript, The Technion, Haifa, Israel.

Lemke, E., Randle, K., and Robertshaw, C. S. Effects of degree of initial acquisition, group size, and general mental ability on concept learning and transfer. *Journal of Educational Psychology*, 1969, *60*, 75–78.

Lew, M. and Bryant, R. The use of cooperative groups to improve spelling achievement for all children in the regular classroom. Paper presented at the Massachusetts Council for Exceptional Children, Boston, 1981.

Lilly, M. S. Improving social acceptance of low sociometric status, low achieving students. *Exceptional Children*, 1971, *28*, 341–347.

Lott, A. J., and Lott, B. E. Group cohesiveness as interpersonal attraction: A review of relationships with antecedent and consequent variables. *Psychological Bulletin*, 1965, *64*, 259–309.

Lucker, G. W., Rosenfield, D., Sikes, J., and Aronson, E. Performance in the interdependent classroom: A field study. *American Educational Research Journal*, 1976, *13*, 115–123.

Madden, N. A., and Slavin, R. E. Cooperative learning and social acceptance of mainstreamed academically handicapped students. *Journal of Special Education*, in press.

Maller J. B. *Cooperation and Competition*. New York: Columbia Teachers College, 1929.

Marquart, D. I. Group problem solving. *Journal of Social Psychology*, 1955, *41*, 103–113.

Martino, L., and Johnson, D. W. The effects of cooperative vs. individualistic instruction on interaction between normal-progress and learning-disabled students. *Journal of Social Psychology*, 1979, *107*, 177–183.

McClintock, E., and Sonquist, J. Cooperative task-oriented groups in a college classroom: A field application. *Journal of Educational Psychology*, 1976, *68*, 588–596.

Meyers, C. E., MacMillan, D. L., and Yoshida, R. K. Regular class education of EMR students, from efficacy to mainstreaming: A review of issues and research. In J. Gottleib (ed.), *Educating Mentally Retarded Persons in the Mainstream*. Baltimore, MD: University Park Press, 1980.

Michaels, J. W. Classroom reward structures and academic performance. *Review of Educational Research*, 1977 *47(1)*, 87–98.

Miller, L. K., and Hamblin, R. L. Interdependence, differential rewarding, and productivity. *American Sociological Review*, 1963, *28*, 768–778.

The effects of segregation and the consequences of desegregation: A social science statement. Appendix to applellant's briefs: Brown vs. Board of Education of Topeka, Kansas. *Minnesota Law Review*, 1953, *37*, 427–439.

Mintz, A. Non-adaptive group behavior. *Journal of Abnormal and Social Psychology*, 1951, *46*, 150–159.

Moreno, J. *Who Shall Survive?* Washington, D.C.: Nervous and Mental Disease Publishing Co., 1934.

Myers, A. Team competition, success, and the adjustment of group members. *Journal of Abnormal and Social Psychology*, 1962, *65*, 325–332.

Oickle, E. A comparison of individual and team learning. Unpublished doctoral dissertation, University of Maryland, 1980.

Peterson, P. L., and Janicki, T. C. Individual characteristics and children's learning in large-group and small-group approaches. *Journal of Educational Psychology*, 1979, *71*, 677–687.

Peterson, P. L., Janicki, T., and Swing, S. Ability x treatment interaction effects on children's learning in largegroup and smallgroup approaches. *American Educational Research Journal*, 1981, *18*, 453–473.

Phillips, B. N., and D'Amico, L. A. Effects of cooperation and competition on the cohesiveness of small face-to-face groups. *Journal of Educational Psychology*, 1956, *47*, 65–70.

Rabbie, J. M., and Horwitz, M. Arousal of ingroup-outgroup bias by chance win or loss. *Journal of Personality and Social Psychology*, 1969, *13*, 269–277.

Raven, B. H., and Eachus, H. T. Cooperation and competition in means-interdependent triads. *Journal of Abnormal and Social Psychology*, 1963, *67*, 307–316.

Richmond, B. O., and Weiner, G. P. Cooperation and competition among young children as a function of ethnic grouping, grade, sex, and reward condition. *Journal of Educational Psychology*, 1973, *64*, 329–334.

Robertson, L. Integrated goal structuring in the elementary school: Cognitive growth in mathematics. Unpublished doctoral dissertation, Rutgers University, 1982.

Rosenbaum, M., Moore, D., Cotton, J., Cook, M., Hieser, R., Shovar, M. N., and Gray, M. Group productivity and process: Pure and mixed reward structures and task interdependence. *Journal of Personality and Social Psychology*, 1980, *39*, 626–642.

Rucker, C. N., Howe, C. E., and Snider, B. The participation of retarded children in junior high academic and non-academic regular classes. *Exceptional Children*, 1969, *26*, 617–623.

Rucker, C. N., and Vincenzo, F. M. Maintaining social acceptance gains made by mentally retarded children. *Exceptional Children*, 1970, *36*, 679–680

Ryack, B. A comparison of individual and group learning of nonsense syllables. *Journal of Personality and Social Psychology*, 1965, *2*, 296–299.

Ryan, F., and Wheeler, R. The effects of cooperative and competitive background experiences of students on the play of a simulation game. *Journal Educational Research*, 1977, *70*, 295–299.

Rynders, J., Johnson, R., Johnson, D. W., and Schmidt, B. Producing positive interaction among Downs Syndrome and nonhandicapped teenagers through cooperative goal structuring. *American Journal of Mental Deficiency*, 1980, *85*, 268–273.

St. John, N. H. *School Desegregation: Outcomes for Children*. New York: John Wiley and Sons, 1975.

Scott, R., and McPartland, J. Desegregation as national policy: Correlates of racial attitudes. *American Educational Research Journal*, in press.

Scott, W. E., and Cherrington, D. J. Effects of competitive, cooperative, and individualistic reinforcement contingencies. *Journal of Personality and Social Psychology*, 1974, *30*, 748–758.

Scranton, T., and Ryckman, D. Sociometric status of learning disabled children in an integrative program. *Journal of Learning Disabilities*, 1979, *12*, 402–407.

Semmel, M., Gottlieb, J., and Robinson, N. Mainstreaming: Perspectives on educating handicapped children in the public schools. In D. Berliner (ed.), *Review of Research in Education*. Washington, D.C.: American Educational Research Association, 1979.

Seta, J., Paulus, P., and Schkade, J. Effects of group size and proximity under cooperative and competitive conditions. *Journal of Personality and Social Psychology*, 1976, *34*, 47–53.

Sharan, S., Ackerman, Z., and Hertz-Lazarowitz, R. Academic achievement of elementary school children in small-group vs. whole class instruction. *Journal of Experimental Education*, 1980, *48*, 125–129.

Sharan, S., Raviv, S., and Kussell, P. Cooperative and traditional classroom learning and the cooperative behavior of seventh-grade pupils in mixed-ethnic classrooms. Unpublished manuscript, University of Tel-Aviv, Israel, 1982.

Sharan, S., and Sharan, Y. *Small-group Teaching*. Englewood Cliffs, NJ: Educational Technology Publications, 1976.

Shattuck, M. Segregation vs. non-segregation of exceptional children. *Journal of Exceptional Children*, 1966, *12*, 235–240.

Sherif, M. *Intergroup conflict and cooperation*. Norman, OK: University of Oklahoma Book Exchange, 1961.

Sherif, M. and Sherif, C. *Groups in harmony and tension*. New York: Harper, 1953.

Siperstein, G., Bopp, M., and Bak, J. Social status of learning disabled children. *Journal of Learning Disabilities*, 1978, *11*, 98–102.

Sirotnik, K. What you see is what you get: A summary of observations in over 1000 elementary and secondary classrooms. Paper presented at the annual convention of the American Educational Research Association, New York, 1982.

Slavin, R. E. Classroom reward structure: Effects on academic performance, social connectedness, and peer norms. Unpublished doctoral dissertation, The Johns Hopkins University, 1975.

Slavin, R. E. Classroom reward structure: An analytic and practical review. *Review of Educational Research*, 1977, *47(4)*, 633–650. (a)

Slavin, R. E. Student learning team techniques: Narrowing the achievement gap between the races. Center for Social Organization of Schools, The Johns Hopkins University, 1977. Report No. 228. (b)

Slavin, R. E. How student learning teams can integrate the desegregated classroom. *Integrated Education*, 1977, *15(6)*, 56–58. (c)

Slavin, R. E. A student team approach to teaching adolescents with special emotional and behavioral needs. *Psychology in the Schools*, 1977, *14(1)*, 77–84. (d)

Slavin, R. E. Separating incentives, feedback, and evaluation: Toward a more effective classroom system. *Educational Psychologist*, 1978, *13*, 97–100. (a)

Slavin, R. E. Student teams and achievement divisions. *Journal of Research and Development in Education*, 1978, *12*, 39–49. (b)

Slavin, R. E. Student teams and comparison among equals: Effects on academic performance and student attitudes; *Journal of Educational Psychology*, 1978, *70*, 532–538. (c)

Slavin, R. E. Effects of biracial learning teams on cross-racial friendships. *Journal of Educational Psychology*, 1979, *71*, 381–387.

Slavin R. E. Effects of student teams and peer tutoring on academic achievement and time on-task. *Journal of Experimental Education*, 1980, *48*, 252–257. (a)

Slavin R. E. *Using Student Team Learning: Revised Edition*. Baltimore, MD: Center for Social Organization of Schools. The Johns Hopkins University, 1980. (b)

Slavin, R. E. Effects of individual learning expectations on student achievement. *Journal of Educational Psychology*, 1980, *72*, 520–524. (c)

Slavin, R. E. A policy choice: Cooperative or competitive learning. *Character*, 1981, *2*, 1–6. (a)

Slavin, R. E. Cooperative learning Changing the normative climate of the classroom. Paper presented at the annual convention of the American Educational Research Association, Los Angeles, 1981. (b)

Slavin, R. E., DeVries, D. L., and Hulten, B. H. Individual vs. team competition: The interpersonal consequences of academic performance. Center for Social Organization of Schools, The Johns Hopkins University, 1975, Report No. 188.

Slavin, R. E. and Karweit, N. Cognitive and affective outcomes of an intensive student team learning experience. *Journal of Experimental Education*, 1981, *50*, 29–35.

Slavin, R. E., and Karweit, N. Student teams and mastery: A factorial experiment in urban Math 9 classes. Paper presented at the annual convention of the American Educational Research Association, New York, 1982.

Slavin, R. E., Leavey, M., and Madden, N. A. Effects of student teams and individualized instruction on student mathematics achievement, attitudes, and behaviors. Paper presented at the annual convention of the American Educational Research Association, New York, 1982.

Slavin, R, E., Madden, N. A., and Leavey, M. Combining cooperative learning and individualized instruction: Effects on the social acceptance, achievement, and behavior of mainstreamed students. Paper presented at the annual convention of the American Educational Research Association, 1982.

Slavin, R. E., and Madden, N. A. School practices that improve race relations. *American Educational Research Journal*, 1979, *16(2)*, 169–180.

Slavin, R. E., and Oickle, E. Effects of cooperative learning teams on student achievement and race relations: Treatment by race interactions. *Sociology of Education*, 1981, *54*, 174–180.

Slavin, R. E., and Tanner, A. M. Effects of cooperative reward structures and individual accountability on productivity and learning. *Journal of Educational Research*, 1979, *72(5)*, 294–298.

Slavin, R. E., and Wodarski, J. S. Effects of student teams and peer tutoring on academic achievement, mutual attraction, and student attitudes. Paper presented at the annual convention of the American Educational Research Association, Toronto, 1978.

Smith, A. J., Madden, H. E., and Sobel, R. Productivity and recall in cooperative and competitive discussion groups. *Journal of Psychology*, 1957, *43*, 193–204.

Spilerman, S. Raising academic motivation in lower class adolescents: A convergence of two research traditions, *Sociology of Education*, 1971, *44*, 103–118.

Stephan, W. G. School desegregation: An evaluation of predictions made in *Brown vs. Board of Education. Psychological Bulletin*, 1978, *85*, 217–238.

Starr, R., and Schuerman, C. An experiment in small-group learning. *The American Biology Teacher*, 1974 (March), 173–175.

Stendler, C., Damrin, D., and Haines, A. C. Studies in cooperation and competition: I. The effects of working for group and individual rewards on the social climate of children's groups. *Journal of Genetic Psychology*, 1951, *79*, 173–197.

Swing, S., and Peterson, P. L. The relationship of student ability and small-group interaction to student achievement. *American Educational Research Journal*, 1982, *19*, 259–274.

Thomas, E. J. Effects of facilitative role interdependence on group functioning. *Human Relations*, 1957, *10*, 347–366.

Thorndike, R. L. On what type of task will a group do well? *Journal of Abnormal and Social Psychology*, 1938, *33*, 409–413.

Webb, N. M. Learning in individual and small group settings. Aptitude research project, School of Education, Stanford University, 1977. Report No. 7.

Webb, N. Group process: The key to learning in groups. *New Directions for Methodology of Social and Behavioral Science: Issues in Aggregation*, 1980, *6*, 77–87.

Webb, N. Group composition, group interaction, and achievement in cooperative small groups. *Journal of Educational Psychology*, in press. (a)

Webb, N. Student interaction and learning in small groups. *Review of Educational Research*, in press. (b).

Webb, N. Peer interaction and learning in cooperative small groups. *Journal of Educational Psychology*, in press. (c)

Webb, N., and Kenderski, C. Student interaction and learning in small group and whole class settings. Paper presented at the Conference on Student Diversity and the Organization, Processes, and Use of Instructional Groups in the Classroom, University of Wisconsin-Madison, May 1982.

Weigel, R. H., Wiser, P. L., and Cook, S. W. Impact of cooperative learning experiences on cross-ethnic relations and attitudes. *Journal of Social Issues*, 1975, *31(1)*, 219–245.

Weiner, B. A. theory of motivation for some classroom experiences. *Journal of Educational Psychology*, 1979, *71*, 3–25.

Weiner, B., and Kukla, A. An attributional analysis of achievement motivation. *Journal of Personality and Social Psychology*, 1970, *15*, 1–20.

Weinstein, A. G. and Holzbach, R. L. Effects of financial inducement on performance under two task structures. The Proceedings, 80th Annual Convention of the American Psychological Association, 1972.

Wheeler, R. Predisposition toward cooperation and competition: Cooperative and competitive classroom effects. Paper presented at the annual convention of the American Psychological Association, San Francisco, 1977.

Wheeler, R., and Ryan, F. L. Effects of cooperative and competitive classroom environments on the attitudes and achievement of elementary school students engaged in social studies inquiry activities. *Journal of Educational Psychology*, 1973, *65*, 402–407.

Workie, A. The relative productivity of cooperation and competition. *Journal of Social Psychology*, 1974, *92*, 225–230.

Young, D. Team learning: An experiment in instructional method as related to achievement. *Journal of Research in Science Teaching*, 1971, *8*, 99–103.

Ziegler, S. The effectiveness of cooperative learning teams for increasing cross-ethnic friendship: Additional evidence. *Human Organization*, 1981, *40*, 264–268.

Index